THE
MILLENNIUM TABLETS

THE QUEST FOR LIGHT

JOHN McINTOSH

ISBN 0-929385-78-0
Published by
Light Technology Publishing
P.O. Box 1526 ✧ Sedona, AZ 86339

Printed by

MISSION
POSSIBLE
COMMERCIAL
PRINTING

P.O. Box 1495 ✧ Sedona, AZ 86339

For all who would bear the light
and show humanity the way to freedom.

Let your light so shine before man that they may see your good
works and glorify your Father which is in heaven.

— Matthew 5:16

ACKNOWLEDGMENTS

This book is dedicated to all the wonderful souls who have personally opened doors of light for me and offered a helping hand over the past twenty years, among them C. Buckle, Ivy Bromfield, Peter Goldman, Russell A. Brown, Mary Ellen Allen, Han Won, Nai Dai, Sebu, and Edith Bruce . . . and to my mother, who opened the first door.

AUTHOR'S NOTE

It could be said that these are the most cataclysmic times in the history of humanity and also the greatest. The capacity for indifference, cruelty, selfishness, abuse and the misuse of power seems limitless, while at the same time there are brilliant pockets of light shining through the darkness everywhere. From environmental crusaders who risk their lives to save the planet to the radiant beings of kindness and charity who serve in the slums and ghettos of the world's worst examples of human suffering, everywhere there are rays of hope. Although each day the world seems to slip toward the abyss of destruction, magnificent examples of courage and selfless love abound in the world.

What is this strange combination of nearly utter darkness and blazing light? As if to mirror the dramatic contradictions of human behavior, Mother Earth moans and shrieks, expelling the poisons of humanity's abuse.

For many who have found the glamour of the world a cold disappointment and who search for deeper meaning in their lives, the rays of dawn are piercing the illusions of the past and revealing a future filled with hope, a future world of peace and love and joy about to be born. And in the final days of the current millennium, together we are experiencing that future's painful delivery.

This story is lovingly offered as encouragement for all who would replace fear and hopelessness with faith, hope and love. It is also a tool to help lessen personal and planetary suffering during this brief transition into the Age of Light.

If it serves as an inspiration for your personal quest for light, pass it on so that others may share your hope and help to lessen humanity's suffering in these final days of darkness.

CONTENTS

INTRODUCTION

DOWN THROUGH THE EONS OF TIME ONLY THE PUREST OF SOULS have been entrusted with keys to the Millennium Tablets, twelve tablets containing powerful secrets. While all the mysteries of the Tablets have been available for study and for use by everyone since the universe was created, only the truest seekers with the most virtuous and courageous hearts have been exposed to the priceless gems of truth in the last ten Tablets.

Many have attained the knowledge in the first tablet. Some have used it wisely to go forward in their quest for freedom, while most have misused the power it gave them, enslaving their fellow humans and causing untold suffering to millions of people down through the ages. Through dedicated pursuit, a few true seekers have opened all the seals, but the Millennium Tablets contain a timed-release lock, scheduled to be opened slowly to give the truths to the mass of humanity at specific times near the end of humankind's journey toward total freedom.

Since the late 1940s the first tablet has been openly revealed and the most perceptive of the human race have publicized and promoted its contents to the world. Much of that unleashed power fanned the flames of the selfish acquisition, greed and human suffering so prevalent on the planet.

Excessive and unbalanced indulgence in the fruits of the material world have pressed down upon humanity causing it to cry out in agony for a deeper purpose for its existence. For those whose inner search and petition have been in true humility, the key to the second tablet has now, during this final decade of the twentieth century, been released.

The last ten years of the century form the most auspicious period in the history of humankind for positive change and for growth toward enlightenment, but they are also the most dangerous, for with the development of light on the planet, there is an equal growth of darkness. Only with a sufficient groundswell in the number of those holding the key to the second Millennium Tablet, those called the lightbearers and wayshowers, could the stage be set for the release of the secrets contained in the other ten tablets and the essence of freedom they embody.

Without the balancing effect derived from the application of the loving guidance of the Tablets during these last critical years of the twentieth century, the forces of darkness and separation that have accumulated throughout the eons of Earth's history will rebound on humankind as Mother Earth cleanses herself in preparation for the Age of Light. That boomerang effect will throw humanity into another dark age and withhold its imminent freedom for another eon.

This is the story of the lightbearers and wayshowers and their vital quest, the quest to establish the balance of light in time for the return swing of the pendulum, a time when the secret of the one hundred forty-four thousand, the number of the saved, will be revealed.

1

A CONFUSING REALITY

THE SILVER-VIOLET BIRD SOARED MAJESTICALLY OVER COASTAL mountain peaks bathed in dusk's purple shroud. From the top of the highest peak, the jet would have appeared to blend almost invisibly into the shimmering twilight sky with only the fiery glow and roar of its engines to reveal its separate identity.

Most of the passengers were sleeping as the final tinge of light descended behind the farthest summit and darkness wrapped its cold embrace around the aircraft. The cabin lights were subdued and all the sun shades were firmly shut.

I had just awakened suddenly from a strange dream in which I had seen myself riding on the top of a giant wave of luminous water. In the distance I could see a sunlike disk on the horizon. As I got closer, I saw that it was divided like a pie into twelve equal pieces. All but one of the pieces was faded, but the last one was a brilliant yellow and it gave me the feeling it was alive. As I stared at the extraordinary object I felt an indescribable sense of urgency and then I clearly heard the voice of a child say the word "millennium." Something about the object was vaguely familiar but I couldn't remember why. The dream seemed to last only a few seconds; then my eyes popped open. I yawned and rubbed my eyes, stretching my neck to get the kinks out, and then switched on my light.

I was sitting in a window seat, with an empty seat to my right, so I decided to peek outside, expecting to see only starlight twinkling in the sky. As I eased the shade slowly upward, I gasped. Outside, an angry red sheet of flames engulfed the aircraft's wing. In shock, I abruptly slammed the shade down. Gathering my courage, I was about to open it again when a friendly greeting distracted my attention.

"Hello. Is this seat taken?" asked a stranger.

I was temporarily disoriented by the shock I had just sustained and could not answer immediately.

"I thought I might find a better seat back here for watching the movie," he said in a warm and friendly manner. "Do you mind if I sit down?"

I relaxed a little and nodded. Somehow, my stress had eased off but not my curiosity, so I stole another quick look out the window. I was surprised but relieved at what I saw — just twinkling stars disturbed only by what appeared to be a short burst of light on a mountain peak immediately below.

"There is nothing but the dead past out there tonight, my friend, but the future looks bright ahead," the stranger said, in a mysterious tone.

Must have been a reflection of the moon, I muttered under my breath, shaking my head and closing the shade.

"Excuse me, I didn't catch what you said."

"Oh, nothing. I must have been half asleep when I looked out the window just before you came along. I thought I saw something odd, that's all." I looked nervously back at the shade.

"My name is Adrian Goodfellow. Thanks for the seat."

"Mine's Jonathan King."

"Yes, I know," Adrian replied.

"You know!" I exclaimed, raising an eyebrow. "How do you know?"

"Oh, I spotted it on your boarding pass in the seat pocket," Adrian answered, pulling the headphone bag from his own seat pocket and tearing it open.

I looked at my boarding pass and saw that it was almost completely submerged in the pocket. I guessed it must have slipped down after he had read my name.

I looked more closely at Adrian. He was of a hard-to-read age, probably somewhere between forty and fifty. He was tall, maybe six feet, two inches, with a strong, lean build like a runner. He wore a loosely hanging white cotton shirt and pants that were also loose-fitting and matched the shirt. He wore brown, comfortable-looking sandals and no socks.

Then I noticed a single piece of jewelry. I couldn't believe my eyes. Within a large silver ring was a piece of turquoise and upon that was a silver circle with pielike cuts in it. It was the same object I had just seen in my dream! I thought I must be imagining things, so I just dismissed it as coincidence until I got a better look at the piece.

I also noticed that Adrian's eyes were a deep, penetrating blue, and dusty blond hair just brushed his shoulders. His face, long and with a square jaw, seemed to move easily and frequently into a warm smile. He looked so relaxed and comfortable that he made me feel very much at ease. This guy could easily be an aging flower-child from the 60s, I mused, and despite the few words that had passed between us I felt a deep sense of strength emanating from Adrian and somehow had a weird feeling that I knew him. I figured that such a feeling must have come from my active imagination which appeared to have been working overtime for the past few moments. In any case, it was certainly nice to have such a pleasant sort of fellow as a companion for the balance of the trip.

Meanwhile, my mouth was feeling dry. The moment I thought of ringing for a flight attendant, one suddenly appeared.

"Well, that certainly was good timing," I exclaimed. "I was just about to push the call button. May I have something to drink please? Do you have apple juice?"

"Yes sir," the attendant replied cheerfully, "but you did push your call button. I saw that your light was on and came right away. I'll be right back, sir."

She was gone in an instant and I was left pondering whether I had indeed pushed the button. I suddenly realized how rude I had been not to ask Adrian if he wanted something. I was just about to apologize when Adrian shrugged his shoulders, laughed and said, "Perhaps she didn't see me."

"How did you know what I was thinking?" I asked in amazement.

"Well, the look of concern on your face said it all," he replied, laughing again.

As Adrian spoke, I picked up an unusual accent.

"Where do you come from, Adrian? I can't seem to place your accent."

"Oh, here and there. Many places, actually. I move around a lot. You might say I'm a citizen of the world," he joked.

I was about to pursue the subject a little further when the cabin lights came on and passengers began to stir in their seats. A voice over the intercom said, "Good morning, ladies and gentlemen. I hope you had a relaxing sleep. In a few moments the flight attendants will be serving a hot breakfast after which we will be showing our in-flight movie, 'Heaven Can Wait.' The captain has suggested you open your window shades, as we are just approaching the Mount of the Holy Cross which, at almost 14,000 feet, is Colorado's highest mountain. Please push the red service button if you require anything at all. Enjoy the view and your breakfast and thank you for your attention."

The aircraft banked slightly, allowing passengers on the opposite side of the cabin from Adrian and me a spectacular view of the mountain peak.

I thought I would go to the lavatory before there was a line, so I excused myself and moved out into the aisle. As I made my way toward the front section of the cabin, I wondered where the time had gone. It seemed the sun had just gone down but already its warm, honey-colored rays were streaming through the many portholes along the aircraft's fuselage. The delicate golden beams seemed to lift everyone's spirits, and I listened to the friendly chatter as I walked down the aisle.

"I must have lost track of time talking to Adrian," I thought as

I turned the knob of the lavatory door. Just as I was entering the tiny cubicle, out of the corner of my eye I caught sight of my new friend in the forward cabin, talking with someone in a nurse's uniform. I jerked to a stop and shook my head. While trying to get a better view, I made an off-balance turn and, wobbling sideways, I fell backwards through the bathroom door and headlong into Adrian's arms! While I was falling, I could hear the sound of his good-natured laughter.

"Whoa, my acrobatic friend. Let the plane do the flying. You haven't got your wings yet, you know," he said as he lifted me to my feet as though I were a feather.

Once I was on my feet, Adrian put his arm around my shoulder to make certain I was steady.

"Where did you come from? I mean, I just left you in your seat a few seconds ago, then I saw you way up at the front of the forward cabin, and now you're here. How?" I pleaded. I began to feel agitated.

"Oh, I noticed you could use a little help and, well, things just sort of happen quickly for me when I want them to. Don't you notice how that sometimes happens to you, too?" He grinned.

I thought back to the coincidental contact with the stewardess earlier but gave little thought to it at that moment, for my attention was on a more pressing need. I turned slightly, moved swiftly back into the little room and closed the door behind me.

"I'll be right back," I blurted out anxiously as the lock clicked shut. I couldn't help noticing how perplexed the face staring back at me in the mirror looked. This is certainly turning out to be a confusing trip, I thought, just as a voice issued from the intercom again.

"Ladies and gentlemen, please return to your seats and fasten your seatbelts, as the captain has informed me we are making our approach to Chicago's O'Hare International Airport."

What in God's name is going on here? I asked myself. We just flew over the Colorado mountains a few minutes ago, we were about to have breakfast and watch a movie and now we're landing in

Chicago. Am I hallucinating? My breath began to come in short gasps, my head began to swim and I blacked out.

2

GENTLE TRANSITION

ADRIAN WAS BENT OVER ME WITH A TENDER AND COMFORTING smile as I blinked and opened my eyes. A throbbing bump on my forehead reminded me that I had fallen against the bathroom counter on my journey into oblivion.

"Where am I?" I groaned.

"Where would you like to be?" Adrian asked merrily in a tone that seemed to my dazed consciousness to be half serious.

"Safely on the ground where I can get my bearings and figure out what in God's name has been going on," I moaned as the thumping in my head increased.

"Well then, if you put it that way, that is precisely where you are, my friend." Adrian grinned, making a light-hearted bow. "Your wish is my command," he chuckled.

I slowly lifted my body into a comfortable sitting position and found that I was on a soft couch in what looked like a paramedical facility. The room was warm and relaxing, with soft lighting and pastel yellow walls that seemed to radiate a feeling of well-being. On a table, a slender crystal vase containing three violet irises gave the room a lovely touch of color.

Adrian offered me a helping hand as I shifted my position, laying his hand on my shoulder as he did so. At that moment the nurse I had seen talking with Adrian in the forward cabin of the aircraft came from behind a screen with a wet cloth and asked me how I was feeling. I was about to answer when a gentle electric shudder moved through my body.

The nurse came over to me and laid the cloth on my head. She smiled sympathetically and repeated her question, ignoring the visible tremor I had just experienced.

"I — I don't really know. A minute ago I thought I was headed for a doozy of a migraine but now the pain seems to be almost gone. I can't explain it, but I'm certainly pleased to be spared the agony. Whenever I get those headaches, they usually last for days."

Adrian and the nurse glanced at each other with a thinly masked look of satisfaction. "Nevertheless, you've sustained a nasty jolt and I feel your body needs a bit of time to balance," Adrian insisted.

The commanding yet gentle manner in which my new friend addressed me surprised and pleased me and gave me a sense of security. It was like the reassurance a loving mother gives to a frightened child. I relaxed and began to slip into a wonderfully pleasant mood of euphoria. I yawned and leaned my head back against the pale yellow wall behind me. The nurse placed a large fluffy pillow behind my head, and I yawned again, feeling even more deeply relaxed, and closed my eyes.

I was just beginning to fall asleep when I slowly opened my eyes, sat up slightly and, sounding heavily sedated, said, "By the waaaay, Mr. Goood . . . felllll . . . oow, I've got a feeew answers that need questioning and I've gaaawt a shuspishun you haf them." With that eloquent statement I tipped my head forward and began to drift into a peaceful sleep.

Adrian gently lifted my head from my chest and repositioned it against the soft pillow. The nurse stroked my hair and fondly kissed my wounded forehead with a sweet smile. Then she and Adrian moved quietly toward the door. A child could not have been tucked into bed with more loving care. I felt relaxed and content as I breathed deeply and let myself become lost in forgetfulness.

✦   ✦   ✦

"He's very confused, as we expected, but I think he'll make the transition very quickly. We've prepared him for this final stage for a very long time, and Jonathan has many fine qualities that will soon emerge. I am certain he will be ready to help us effectively to introduce the second Millennium Tablet to the world," Adrian said with quiet confidence.

Cindy, his assistant, smiled in agreement and replied, "I am very much looking forward to my part of the work with him. I think the way we have planned it will turn the tide in time." She closed the door and hung a sign on it that read

> Jonathan King
> The Millennium Tablets
> Transition

They walked away from the room and made their way up the aisle of the aircraft. Adrian was dressed in a captain's uniform and Cindy wore a cabin attendant's uniform. As they moved among the returning vacationers, they exchanged friendly greetings, commented on the wonderful tans passengers had gotten while vacationing in Hawaii, and asked questions about points of interest they had seen.

One inebriated traveler asked, with a mockingly haughty gesture, "Hey, Captain, who's flying this thing, anyhow?"

A frowning lady with thin lips, a sallow complexion and a permanent worry furrow on her brow looked on from the seat beside him.

"Oh don't worry, sir," Adrian laughed, looking directly into the anxious woman's eyes. "This plane no longer requires flying." He patted her on the shoulder and she immediately relaxed. Her husband, however, began to appear very distraught, an unfamiliar feeling for a man who had preyed on his wife's delicate nature for years.

"For goodness' sake, Harold, what in heaven's name is wrong with you, anyway? The nice captain said everything is okay, so everything is okay. Right, Captain Goodfellow?"

Adrian nodded with a grin.

"They are probably all run by computers or something, so stop your fussing and relax, you ninny." When she stopped speaking her eyes opened wide and a slow, satisfying smile spread across her face. The bold, commanding manner in which she had just addressed her bullying husband shocked and pleased her at the same time.

If Harriet had ever spoken to Harold in that tone before he would have immediately gone into a rage and shouted her down as if she'd been a worm. However, at that moment he felt only like throwing up.

Cindy appeared out of nowhere with a glass of bubbling liquid and said, "Drink this right down, Mr. Baker, and you'll feel a whole lot better in a few seconds."

Harold was unaccustomed to taking orders of any kind, but he found himself immediately obeying the stewardess. He swallowed the contents of the glass and a few seconds later closed his eyes and went to sleep.

As his eyes were closing, Cindy winked at Harriet and took the empty glass from his hand as his arm fell to his lap. Harriet Baker smiled at Cindy with a victorious glint in her eyes, as if to say, Hooray.

Meanwhile, passengers bustled up and down the aisle, used the lavatory, removed items from the overhead compartments, rang for cabin service and in general acted as airline passengers normally act on a normal flight.

The intercom sounded its tone. "Ladies and gentlemen, this is Captain Goodfellow speaking. In a few moments we will be making our final approach to Chicago's O'Hare International Airport. Please fasten your seatbelts, return your trays to the seat in front of you, adjust your seatbacks to the upright position and be certain all your carry-on luggage is safely stowed under the seat in front of you or in the overhead bins. When we reach the terminal building, I ask you to follow the flight attendants to a special information area."

The passengers anxiously began to question each other about what the captain might have meant by a special information area. Some nervously whispered concern about some sort of terrorist at-tack at the airport, but the stewardesses circulating throughout the cabin assured them that in fact there had recently been an airline disaster and that the emergency measure was for their comfort and convenience.

Twenty minutes later the plane touched down in Chicago. Soon the weary travelers disembarked and were divided into groups according to their seat numbers. They moved through corridors that further subdivided the groups until finally each had found his way into a private room that had been specially prepared. Through a speaker in each cubicle, further instructions were broadcast. "Thank you for your cooperation in following these unusual procedures. We are certain some of you are asking yourselves why such elaborate arrangements have been made for you. You will notice there is a comfortable chair directly in front of a television set and VCR. Please make yourselves comfortable, relax, and when you are ready, press the play button on the VCR. Soon everything will become clear to you. We apologize for any inconvenience this might have caused you."

Some passengers were intrigued by the efficient manner in which the airport authorities had handled the disaster. Others were irritated, realizing they would miss connections or appointments, while most just felt it was some sort of normal procedure in emergency situations and dutifully complied with the instructions given.

Eventually, I awoke. I felt so rejuvenated it was as if I had slept for a week. It was strange, though, that I did not feel the least bit hungry. After a long sleep I usually had a ravenous appetite.

That thought crossed my mind only momentarily before incredible scenes began to appear on the screen before me. As I watched intently, I became more deeply bewildered. There would be many more questions for my mysterious new friend.

3

REUNION

"WOULD YOU LIKE TO GO FOR A STROLL ALONG THE BEACH, MR. Jonathan?" a familiar laughing voice inquired from behind me as I stared transfixed at the television transmission.

"Huh? What's that?" I jumped, my concentration broken. I swung around to find Adrian grinning and dressed in a pair of bright, flowery swim trunks. Around his neck was draped a white towel, the kind of beach towel hotels provide for their guests. Other than thong sandals, that was all he wore, showing off the body of a trim young athlete. I had to accept yet another version of my friend's chameleon-like nature, for no cosmetics or Hollywood makeover could have hidden the fact that Adrian had every appearance of being no more than twenty-five years of age. I was in a state of shock and yet for some inexplicable reason that I couldn't fathom, I took in the whole surprise as if it were completely normal.

God, I really must have suffered a serious blow to my head, I agonized to myself.

"I see that I have caught you off guard again, my friend," he laughed. "I bet you didn't think I had the nerve to wear such a flashy pair of swim trunks, did you?" Adrian chuckled and continued to avoid addressing my real concern.

"Swim trunks!" I meekly replied. My tranquilized state stifled what should have been a more dramatic show of frustration. Before I could adequately verbalize that concern, Adrian had me on my feet and out the door.

As the two of us left my room, the door swung shut and I noticed a sign on it that read

> Jonathan King
> The Millennium Tablets
> Indoctrination

Immediately outside the door a short corridor led to a dusty road lined with palm trees.

Harriet Baker sat sobbing her heart out as if a lead weight had mysteriously been lifted from her. On the screen before her was her mother, also crying, as she pleaded with her daughter for understanding. "Harriet, honey, I didn't know. I just didn't know. I tried the best I knew how to protect you and bring you up after your father passed away and left us alone. His death almost destroyed me. I just relied on him so much.

"I became terrified of losing you, too, so I smothered you and taught you my fear. I sheltered you from making friends I thought might hurt you. I steered you away from taking chances so you wouldn't have to face failure and be disappointed by life the way I had been. I encouraged you not to be too assertive so that you wouldn't offend people.

"But for all my care and protection, you became indecisive and weak, and your reward for being an attentive, obedient daughter was a life of suppression, intimidation and humiliation. I exposed you to years of emotional suffering and the loss of your self-worth."

Harriet's mother went on and on, explaining detail after detail, tearing away years of misunderstanding, confusion and failure and allowing Harriet to comprehend her many disappointments in life. While there was remorse for many opportunities that had passed her by, Harriet began to experience a growing sense of relief and a profound revelation that her life could be different and better, much better. The fact that her mother, who had been dead for more than twenty years, had been carrying on an interactive audio-visual conversation with her for over an hour had so far escaped her notice.

✦   ✦   ✦

Together, Adrian and I silently padded along a beautiful stretch of deserted beach. Adrian had given me a comfortable pair of turquoise bathing trunks that matched the crystal-clear waters within the boundaries of a great coral reef lying a few hundred yards offshore. I was bursting with questions but somehow felt compelled to wait for Adrian to initiate the conversation. Finally, he began.

"So, my friend, you're looking much better — refreshed, revitalized, ready for adventure."

"Adventure? Ready for adventure?" I remarked sarcastically. "You think I'm ready for adventure, do you? Do you have any conceivable idea what I've been through since I met you? Do you know that just before you came along, I thought I saw the entire wing of the aircraft in a sheet of flames? Ever since then it's been one confusing adventure after another, not the least of which is this walk along a secluded tropical beach with you when we are supposed to be in Chicago." I raised my arms in frustration.

"Yes, Jonathan, I know," Adrian replied softly as he led me to a cluster of volcanic boulders worn almost smooth by the incessant wash of the tide. Wide mats of white hinahina flowers covered the soft pink sand around the giant rocks. Waves lapped rhythmically at our feet. Gulls circled and dove, crying out in hungry repartee while a warm and gentle breeze wafted by, filled with a delightful but unknown fragrance. My frustration began to ease a bit as the calming environment massaged my tension.

"What you are experiencing at this moment, my confused friend, is what your science fiction writers might call an energy field. You feel it as a deep sense of calm, a peaceful blending of clear awareness that buffers the chaos swirling within your mind. This wonderful feeling is accompanied by a churning sensation right here in your solar plexus." Adrian pointed to my midsection and smiled sweetly.

"There is an anxiety to get on with it, whatever it is. You feel confused, uncomfortable and tight. Naturally, you find this condition contradictory. Your whole system seems turned upside down and yet somehow you have a sense of tranquillity. Unknown to you, at this moment you have been distracted from events that have caused trauma to your bodies."

I wondered which comment seemed the most implausible and disturbing. What could possibly be more traumatic than what I had so far experienced? I shuddered at the unwelcome prospect of finding out. And what did Adrian mean by "bodies"? There had been only one face in the mirror the last time I'd checked, even though I had blacked out shortly afterwards. I had to laugh to myself as the irony of that thought passed through my mind.

While I was pondering these enigmas, Adrian had picked up a piece of driftwood and was sketching something in the sand near my feet. He had drawn a little stick figure and wrapped larger and larger circles around the effigy, like baggy overcoats, until there were seven, including the body. Then he began to explain.

"A human being is virtually blind to all there is to see, his range of vision encompassing only a tiny speck on a scale that includes many thousands of more highly refined vibrations. Some of the better-known ones are X rays, ultraviolet rays and radio waves. There are also many others well beyond the boundaries of man's limited physical eye."

I suppose I was aware that science had developed specialized instrumentation that could not only identify and separate many of these waves or rays but could also enable scientists to perceive many aspects of reality for the first time. For example, many distant stars still invisible to conventional high-powered telescopes had been revealed through the use of sophisticated radio-wave telescopes.

Adrian continued as he pointed his driftwood stick at imaginary objects in the air. "The fact that this or that so-called phenomenon cannot be recorded by the naked human eye does not eliminate or diminish in any way its existence."

The tension in my stomach began to fade and my shoulders started to relax. I eased more fully into the peaceful energy field, or whatever it was, and listened with growing fascination, content for the time being to wait for the answers I sought.

"Einstein saw that there were really no such things as solids, just atoms and molecules in constant movement, existing more or less close to each other. Some atoms seem to move very slowly when viewed from your normal perspective and those atoms can be seen to form solids or liquids. Most, however, move much more quickly and can be seen only by those with a highly developed visual sense. For example, the lovely aroma that you have been wondering about since we began our stroll has always been there, but until now you have not been able to tune in to its frequency and enjoy it through your human sense of smell."

Adrian kept speaking as if he knew exactly what I was thinking. I found it disturbing and despite my relaxed mood, I anxiously wished he would clear up the mystery surrounding his abnormal behavior.

I'd considered the possibility that I might be hallucinating and left that possibility open for the time being. Naturally, it had also occurred to me by then that I might be dreaming, but I had almost dismissed that idea since no dream I could remember had ever seemed to last so long or be so vivid. From articles I had read on the subject, I knew that records of brain activity indicated that the dream state never lasted as long as the dreamer thought it did, but what I was experiencing would certainly be considered a record-breaking dream in terms of time.

On the other hand, I'd also read that time often became compressed in the dream state, and I knew that was true because of an experience I'd had once. I had awakened at my normal time of 6:00 a.m., which was clearly visible on my bedside alarm clock. It was a Sunday so I pushed the snooze button and went back to sleep to catch twenty winks. I awoke to the clock's buzzer precisely at 6:20 a.m. after a dream that seemed to have lasted for hours.

So perhaps I really was asleep and dreaming, still seated in the aircraft and having a graphically vivid dream that was seeming to last for days. What else could explain all the strange things that were happening? Anyway, that was my best guess at the time.

Adrian seemed to be watching me as if he were following my train of thought. Then he smiled knowingly and continued with his explanation.

"Consider your thoughts. For eons, great minds have repeated the same truth: 'Thoughts are living things'; 'Energy follows thought'; 'You become what you think about'; 'You attract what you think about'; 'You reap what you sow' and so on."

Adrian stood and we strolled along the water's edge as the surf flowed in and out. The sun's rays on my back energized me with new vitality as the steady syncopation of the lapping water seemed to drain the last vestige of tension from my body. It was as if Mother Nature were performing a mysterious and subtle healing on me. I could not explain the feeling exactly but nevertheless, I benefited from its magic. My steps were light and effortless even though I was walking in wet sand that gave under my weight, and surprisingly, my legs and ankles felt absolutely no fatigue.

"If all the things that I have thus far shared with you are true, then it should be possible, under the right circumstances and with elevated vision, so to speak, to actually see thoughts, shouldn't it? They would appear the same as solids do to a less developed pair of eyes."

I instinctively reeled back mentally as a habitual sense of pragmatism rejected his theory. Even considering the lack of scientific evidence to explain the many events I had been through and even considering the possibility that I was dreaming, my common sense rebelled against the possibility that thoughts could be visible. But if Adrian felt my skepticism or saw it on my face, he was apparently unperturbed since he continued with his line of reasoning.

"Most people will readily admit they have felt a force or a feeling of discomfort at the back of their necks only to discover on turning around that someone was staring at them, often from a considerable distance away. Others will testify that on entering the home of strangers, before having met with them or having learned any details concerning their character or habits, they have sensed a mood or feeling of cold uneasiness or perhaps, conversely, one of warm friendliness."

Adrian seemed to be methodically weaving a fabric with his conversation, one strand at a time, adding textures and colors as he went. Obviously, he knew exactly where he was going and what the cloth would look like, but I didn't have a clue. Nevertheless, I was enjoying his company and the wonderful new feeling that was creeping over me as we walked, so I didn't really care if I understood where it was going or not. I decided to just let go and reserve judgment for later.

"Now let us pose a hypothetical situation." He grinned as his voice picked up tempo. "Let us say that it really is possible to move beyond or to move above the so-called normal range of vision, the sight that comprehends material things as being only solid or liquid. Let us assume we can step-up our vision to see faster-moving molecules, those perhaps at the level of gases and other clouds of vapor or even higher.

"Now suppose we apply a color to these quicker vibrations in order to give them individual identity. For example, red molecules might mean either anger or intense emotion while green could be considered helpful and uplifting. The color rose might be interpreted to mean love, and so on."

The thought of the color rose brought instantly to my mind a beautiful face from my distant past. It flashed quickly before my inner eye, then disappeared.

Adrian had stopped walking and was printing the names of the colors he had mentioned in the wet sand at our feet as he repeated his theoretical labels for them.

"Now suppose, as we continue our walk along the shore, that we should spy in the distance the form of someone approaching. As yet, the person is too far away for us to perceive whether or not he or she is known to us, but with our newly elevated sense of sight we behold a beautifully colored outline shimmering around the body."

Adrian had once again drawn his little seven-coated stick figure in the smooth sand and he paused while I pondered his words. I just looked on, wondering what to expect next and still perplexed about the purpose of my friend's dissertation. As we raised our heads, Adrian began to walk slowly ahead of me. I was about to follow, but what I saw made my jaw drop open. My feet remained cemented in the wet sand.

Adrian slowed his easy pace and looked over his shoulder with an expression of delight on his face. "It might even be possible to sense or feel or know who the stranger is by awakening a long-forgotten memory of the distinctive color patterns belonging to the person."

Tears of joy streamed down my face. My heart seemed to rise up into my throat. My body shuddered with anticipation but still I could not move. I ached to cry out but somehow choked it back. Soon, however, I was unable to retain the growing mixture of delirious anxiety and blissful suspense.

Adrian was at my side in a flash and he put his arm around my shoulders. The calming effect of his touch was instantaneous and I slumped to the wet sand like jelly, propping myself up in a half-sitting position.

In the distance, on the isolated stretch of beach we had been walking, a human form was beginning to take shape. Surrounding it was an unmistakable rosy glow intermingled with other pastel shades of violet and yellow. Using only my normal vision, I could not possibly have known who the approaching figure was from such a distance; however, I continued to experience a deep emotional connection that was unmistakable.

Adrian sat down beside me and spoke to me in a soft low tone. "I think an old friend from your past has come to see you, my friend."

"It's . . . it's Diana, Sister Diana. Oh God, I can't believe it. I thought she was only a childhood dream." I moaned and buried my face in my hands, letting myself fall head first into the sand and sobbing with joy as the pent-up emotion poured out of me like a river. I had lived through a similar scene many years before and the wonderful feelings I'd experienced then came flooding back to me.

In a few minutes I regained my composure and lifted myself up to a sitting position. Adrian said nothing but kept a watchful eye on me as the vision from my past advanced closer. By then the figure could easily be seen as she gracefully glided toward the two of us. She had long silky auburn hair that hung straight down to her waist. Around her slender body she wore a gaily printed wrap like those worn on the Hawaiian islands by the native girls. A single coral-colored blossom rested in her hair on the left side. Her face was angelically peaceful, innocent and lovely. She had a delicate smile and soft doelike eyes with lids that half covered an exquisite deep green hue that radiated light and suggested a great depth of silent power.

My memory was swiftly returning and I recalled how uplifting those shining eyes had so often felt to the lonely little orphan boy I had once been.

She moved fluidly, in perfect harmony with the ebb and flow of the ocean rhythms. Finally, she was directly in front of me, and the light that I had seen surrounding her in the distance enveloped both of us and somehow seemed to lift me to my feet.

The light was a pink glow with a violet tinge. Shimmering blues and indigos ribboned through her upper body while waves of sea green blended with golden-yellow threads in her lower body. As she approached to within a step of me the unusual fragrance that Adrian and I had enjoyed during our stroll began to intensify. I didn't remember ever before having experienced such wonderfully intoxicating perfume.

4

THE GREAT WHITE SISTERHOOD

INDELIBLY BEAUTIFUL MEMORIES FILLED MY MIND AS ONCE AGAIN tears of joy filled my eyes. I saw myself as a lonely, frightened little boy, abandoned by my parents when I was only five years old. One day I was joyfully playing at my favorite pastime, building sand-castles at the seashore, and next thing I knew I was a prisoner in a sad dark room.

A single rickety table stood beside my tiny cot. There was a big wooden cross hanging on the dingy gray wall at the foot of that uncomfortable bed, and a brown suitcase sat by itself under an empty and rusting clothing rack.

The big people were cold and stern and there were rules, lots of silly rules. For example, there were rules about when to eat, when to sleep, when to speak and what to say when you did speak, and special clothes that had to be neat. There were chores to do and classes to attend, and always there was loneliness. Surrounded by many, the little lad that I was felt very lonely.

Why did Momma and Papa desert me? I thought. What had I done that was so bad that I deserved to be in this terrible place? Why couldn't I just go home and have things be the way they used to be?

As the days turned into months, that orphaned boy withdrew deeper and deeper inside his forlorn little world. The big strict lady that everybody obeyed had told me that my parents had had to go away and that I must be a big man and learn to do without them.

Maybe someday, if I were really, really good and did everything I was told to, maybe I would see them again. My heart was cold and as tight as a clenched fist when I recalled those horrible months before Sister Diana came to me.

But then that wonderful spring morning streamed brightly into my memory and I began to relax again. My breathing slowed to a gentle rhythm as I drifted into a heavenly reverie.

One morning I had awakened earlier than usual, before the five o'clock bells tolled. I'd rubbed the sleep from my half-opened eyes, yawned and sat up to peer through the darkness at a beautiful rosy glow at the foot of my bed. Standing there was a lovely lady in a pure white nun's habit. She was surrounded by a shimmering rose-colored hue with a violet tinge.

Years later I dismissed that vision and others like it as the foolish imaginings of an introverted, lonely little boy no one would believe, but at the time they seemed very real.

I was not at all afraid, so I asked her what her name was and she said she was Sister Diana of the Great White Sisterhood and that she was there to be my friend. She was very different from the big people with the black-and-white uniforms, who often seemed so strict.

Over the months that followed, Sister Diana came to visit me every day. We would walk in the woods near the big building in which I lived. She seemed to know every tree, every shrub and every plant and could even talk to the animals as they came and trustfully ate out of her hand. It seemed the whole forest was her friend.

She told me never to tell anyone about her visits, but one day when the big lady in charge of all the ladies in black-and-white uniforms cruelly scolded me for carelessly dropping my dinner plate during grace, I blurted out in anger, "Leave me alone, you terrible old witch, or I'll tell my friend Sister Diana and she'll come and take me away from this awful place." There was no Sister Diana at the orphanage, so the children all laughed at me and I ran away to my room in tears.

From that moment on the other children teased me and taunted me and the big ladies in black-and-white uniforms told me I was ungrateful and that I was never again to lie and make up bad stories like that or I would be sent away, and then I'd really be sorry. Since no one had ever seen me with Sister Diana, some of the ladies in the black-and-white uniforms would shake their heads and say I was deranged and addled and there was little hope for that poor unhappy fellow no one seemed to be able to reach.

So I withdrew even more within myself. Sister Diana was my only friend. She would come and hold me in her arms and tell me wonderful stories about the world outside and all the places I would one day explore.

Most of the ladies in black and white had tried their best to make me feel welcome, but after the accident I had never come out of myself. There was a mental block as solid as a wall that was my shield, my protection from disappointment. And from memory. I had no recollection of the car swerving on the oil-slick mountain road. It had gone over the side of a cliff and thrown me through an open window, leaving me unconscious by the roadside. The authorities could not locate any other family members, so I was sent to the nuns' orphanage.

I was put into the mainstream of normal activities by the nuns and I followed the schedules and obeyed the rules but never learned to get along with any of the other children or to do anything more than the minimum that was asked of me. The other little boys and girls whispered about me, saying I talked to myself in the nearby woods during playtime. Eventually, one of the nuns overheard their stories and decided to follow me into the woods one day. Hiding behind a large tree, she watched me sitting on a stump looking up at thin air and talking, so she thought, to no one. She sadly shook her head and without listening, turned and crept away in silence.

Despite my isolation, Sister Diana's love and companionship made life bearable, even bright and happy at times, and I longed for her visits.

Then one day she came to my room with a very serious-looking smile on her beautiful face. She told me I would soon be going away to live with a distant relative of my parents, an aunt and uncle who had lived in Europe and had recently moved to a lovely home in California. They had just heard about my being in an orphanage and wanted me to come and live with them by the sea. I would have lots of little friends and a beach to play on again. I would be happy and I would never again be lonely.

I immediately began jumping up and down and shouting for joy. Sister Diana smiled and held her finger to her lips to indicate I should not celebrate too loudly. So I yelled in a whisper and gleefully, in my innocence, asked if they had room for her too. Would she be coming with me? Would she visit me the way she always had?

Sister Diana smiled sadly at me and said she would be there soon but that she had many other duties and had to be faithful to those who counted on her as I had. There were many other little boys and girls just like me who would be very sad if she didn't visit them as she had visited me.

I dropped slowly to my little cot. I covered my face with my hands and began to sob. "But I love you, Sister Diana. You are my best friend, my only friend. Please don't leave me! Please don't leave me," I cried.

"Bless you, my little angel," she cooed. "I will never desert you. One day I will come to you when you are all grown up and we will walk and talk as we have here. Then I will show you many things that are important to your destiny." She laughed, opening her arms as if holding the world in them. I giggled at the gesture and jumped into her waiting embrace.

Several months later when I was playing quietly by myself on the beach behind my aunt and uncle's seaside home, I saw a rosy-pink glow in the distance. Soon Sister Diana was beside me, kneeling in the sand next to a huge sandcastle I had just finished constructing.

I was so happy my wonderful Sister Diana was with me again. We walked and talked, we played in the sand and sang songs together all day long. Then at the end of the day we walked along the beach hand in hand, together.

My small hand clenched hers as if I would never again let it go. She asked me if I would like to play a special game and I immediately jumped up and down and yelled in delight.

"Oh yes, yes. Let's play a game." I stopped and thought for a moment, then asked, "Which game do you wanna play? Hide-and-go-seek? Marbles? Yeah! How about marbles? I've got a bag of king-sized marbles and I'll even let you borrow some, if you like. But I'd hafta give you a chance on a counta I'm real good at it." I grinned and then laughed sheepishly, lowering my head as I blushed.

"Why Jonathan, I believe you are bragging," Sister Diana said with a laugh. "It's good, my little angel, to be proud of your abilities and I am happy to see you smile about your accomplishments. But one day I will explain how you are not alone in those accomplishments; then your pride will become a very important thing called humility. It is indeed a very powerful thing to have, and one day you will possess it."

I nodded my head in an attempt to act grown up and wise like Sister Diana, but I didn't really understand. She knew this, of course, and smiled at me, knowing the value of planting a seed which, in a happy and fertile mind that feels loved and cared for, was sure to yield its full harvest in due season.

"No, my little friend, this very special game must be played only by the most serious players in all the world. Do you think you could be one of those kinds of players?" she asked in a very solemn tone.

"Oh yes!" I exclaimed eagerly. "I will be very serious if it's a game I can play with you, Sister."

"All right then, this game is like hide-and-go-seek except I call it hide-and-go-find," she explained, "because you must be very observant and pay close attention in order to find me."

We continued walking at the edge of the water, sinking in the wet sand as the waves rolled in and out, and as we walked we swung our arms back and forth in childlike abandon while we splashed in the water.

She paused for a moment and I asked, "Why must I pay such close attention? Why can't I just look for you?"

"To find me you must pay very close attention because I will be hidden in a very special way," she replied. "As you are growing up you will not see me as I now appear but in many disguises."

"Oh, that does sound like fun," I chirped. "But what if I don't know it's you? Will you tell me?"

"That's why you must be very alert and become my little detective. Because in this special game you will know it's me only when your heart tells you so. Always listen to your heart, my little friend. It will never lie to you. This is the most important lesson I have ever taught you, so listen again. Your heart will never lie to you!"

I squinted my eyes and puckered up my mouth as if I were trying to force the lesson into my head.

"But can't you give me a little hint where you will be so I don't miss you? I would be very sad if I couldn't find you."

Sister Diana considered this request for a moment, then replied, "When you were in the nuns' care and felt very sad and lonely even though they tried their best to cheer you up and be your friend, what was it that made you happy?"

"That's easy!" I cried. "It was you, Sister Diana. It was because you were my friend. That's what made me happy."

"Yes, that is true, but I really did nothing that the nuns could not have done," she said, gently leading me to my own conclusion.

"Oh, but you did, Sister Diana. You loved me. They just took care of me," I replied with certainty.

"The sisters did love you by taking care of you. They just didn't know how to get inside your heart because your heart was so wounded by the thought that your parents had deserted you. The nuns were afraid to tell you your parents had died because they thought you might fall even more deeply inside yourself and then they would never be able to reach you and help you to grow up happy and strong. They did what they thought was right. But I told you the truth. Remember? After that you cried and cried for a long time until finally your heart began to heal and the hurt started to go away."

I listened carefully and in my childish way began to feel guilty about the way I had acted toward the sisters at the orphanage. I wished I could tell them I was much better and thank them for their kindness.

Sister Diana picked up the thread of my mood and squeezed my little hand tenderly. "I'm sure the sisters knew how difficult things were for you and understood. Their love for all children is very great indeed and sometimes when unfortunate little children like you with special problems come into their care, they are a little stricter than parents so the children will grow up independent and able to stand on their feet sooner."

"Do you mean, Sister Diana, that I will find you in my heart?" I inquired with surprisingly mature insight, pointing to my chest as I asked.

"Very good, my little angel. But it will be much more than that. When you feel love or kindness in others or in yourself, you will know that I am with you. And remember, love comes in many different disguises, which you will discover as you grow older, so you must look closely." She looked down at me with a glowing smile of approval at my youthful grasp of the game ahead of us. I am sure she wondered with concern if my interest would stand the test of time without her physical presence to remind me of the game.

Then, as the gravity of the game began to dawn on me, I asked, "Does that mean I won't be with you like this again, Sister Diana?" My chest began to heave as the sadness welled up within me. The thought of parting with my beloved friend was more than my little heart could bear. We sat down on the sand and I laid my head on Sister Diana's lap as the tears began to flow.

She stroked my hair and softly hummed a soothing lullaby she had sung many times before during our forest walks. Soon I calmed down and drifted into a semisleep as Sister Diana whispered something in my ear. "My little angel, someday we shall once again sit on a beach together like this and walk and talk, and I will help to lead you to your destiny." As she said those prophetic words to me, she gently slipped something into my pocket. It was a flat gold stone in the shape of a triangle with the figures MT-I etched into it.

At that moment, the vision of Sister Diana and the little boy I had been faded from the screen within my mind. The sunlike disk I had seen in my dream while on the aircraft appeared in my inner sight. Suddenly I realized that the little gold stone was a piece of the disk, the brilliant gold piece that had seemed to be alive.

In the years that followed my last meeting with Sister Diana, the gold stone had become a sort of amulet I held in my hand whenever I was using my imagination on something that was challenging me. But what was the connection between the stone and the disk?

My eyes blinked and the vision vanished. I knew Sister Diana had kept her promise to me. And the sense of urgency I had felt when I'd first seen the sunlike disk was with me again, and it stayed with me. Deep within my heart I sensed that a compelling mystery concerning the gold stone was about to be unraveled for me.

5

HUMANITY'S DESTINY

THE SILENT GATHERING OF WHITE-CLOAKED FIGURES KNELT BEFORE
a large sunlike disk that hung at the far end of an alabaster hall. The
figures were not worshipping the disk but paying respect to the
wisdom it symbolized. In the ceiling of the room was a similar disk
constructed of violet glass and framed in gold. A six-pointed star lay
within the circle and within that was a cross. A bright white light
shone at a slight angle through the glass, casting a duplicate of the
design on the altar before the sunlike disk. It was the only light
shining into the room and yet a rosy golden hue filled the entire
structure. The hall was suffused with a gently penetrating sense of
peace that suggested nothing could disturb it, and soft, sweet music
drifted like a ribbon through the room. Everything radiated the
essence of tranquillity.

A majestic figure glided toward the altar. His cloak was violet
with a golden braid around the neck and a thin golden rope around
the waist. He had a boyish appearance combined with a depth of
wisdom that suggested ancient knowledge dwelt within his consciousness. Power moved with his every step and when he spoke his
voice resonated the pure essence of love.

"I, Sankumi, address you now, my fellow servants of the Great
White Brotherhood and Sisterhood. For eons of time we have pro-
jected our focus on the wave of light now fast approaching Mother
Earth. Soon all life on Earth will begin to feel the beneficent changes

necessary for the transition into the Age of Light due to occur in the next millennium.

"The first Millennium Tablet has just been revealed to all of humanity and will filter into the mainstream of life over the next forty years. At the end of that period, the second Millennium Tablet will be opened to the world and the final countdown will begin as the world emerges from its cocoon and humanity spreads its fragile wings to fly to its true destiny.

"This is the vision we have held for the future. However, the accumulated darkness of humanity's history now bears heavily down upon it and the forces of evil are conscious of their imminent loss of power over the material world. For thousands of years we have anticipated the rebellion this would cause, but we could not predict how powerful the conflict would be, since humans have the gift of free will. We now realize it will take the greatest commitment of our combined forces of light together with the light of the emerging lightbearers and wayshowers on Earth who will serve as apprentices to us during the last few critical years before the millennium.

"For this reason we have searched for and found a suitable candidate who will be prepared to lead the quest for light on the Earth plane during the final decade before the century's end. This soul will be the focal point toward whom we will pour our energies in order to harvest the true servers of humanity into the fold of lightbearers and wayshowers. Our dedicated focus now is to work together with that band of worthy brothers and sisters to bring in the Age of Light with the least amount of suffering by humanity and to stave off the real danger that now exists of delaying the Age of Light for another eon. To assist us with this monumental task, there are three amongst us whom we have chosen to oversee the work on the Earth plane of lifting the consciousness of the chosen soul to a level where he can safely be exposed to the energy and power of all twelve tablets and can therefore be a suitable instrument through which we can focus our light during the final years of tribulation on Earth."

The three stood before Sankumi at the altar. Sankumi and the entire assembly knelt in silent prayer to the Great Spirit that their work would be successful and that humanity would safely emerge on the other side of the transformational period and there take the final step toward total freedom and their true destiny.

6

CREATING

I HAD NO IDEA HOW LONG I HAD BEEN RELIVING THOSE PRECIOUS times with Sister Diana. It felt like hours had passed, and I was about to apologize for daydreaming and for greeting my dear old friend with so little regard, when Sister Diana spoke. "Time has no meaning here, dear friend. Everything is now. However, by your reckoning I have only just arrived, so you need not feel I have been kept waiting."

I didn't understand all she had said and in any case felt she was just being kind, but I let go of my embarrassment with an awkward chuckle and then laughed out loud as my mood changed. "God, what's wrong with me, anyway?"

As I blurted out the words, I threw my arms around my long-lost friend. We embraced for a long time, then parted a few inches, looked into each other's eyes and smiled with deep mutual affection. I thought I saw a tear in Sister Diana's eye as the love I'd forgotten about for so long once again radiated from them.

Adrian had been standing at a respectable distance but now took a step toward the two of us and piped in, with mock offense, "Hey, you two, what about me? I need love too, you know!" The way he said it reminded me of a puppy extending a little paw with a meek look to get attention from its master. All three of us broke into uproarious laughter. By the time we stopped we were all lying on our backs in the sand, holding our stomachs.

Finally Sister Diana managed to say something. "I think, dearheart, that you have put me on the back shelf of your mind all these years in favor of what you considered to be more important matters."

I sat up abruptly and started to protest but was distracted by the view of the wide horizon. In the distance swollen storm clouds dumped their contents into the ocean while a short distance away, a perfect semicircular rainbow poured its palette of living color into the sea. The air was warm and a welcome breeze carried to me the lovely new fragrance that surrounded my two friends. Seagulls circled and soared high above us in the bright blue sky while a solitary pelican dive-bombed with precision into an imaginary bull's eye, targeting its lunch.

And now Sister Diana, wonderful Sister Diana, was back in my life, along with my mysterious new friend Adrian. I felt so good. Life, whatever it held in store for me, was heavenly at that moment. As I turned around to speak, Adrian and Sister Diana were smiling with that discerning look I had come to recognize.

I couldn't put my finger on it, but I sensed that a great change in my life was imminent. I could feel the undeniable presence of something that had always been waiting for me. It was waiting and calling out to me in a still, small voice and it spoke of a choice I would soon have to make. The sunlike disk, the gold stone amulet and my friends all had something to do with it. But what? The impression was like the thundering hooves of a distant band of approaching horses pounding out a mysterious code.

My two friends nodded their heads as if to acknowledge the truth of what I was feeling. I was beginning to get used to the idea that Adrian could react to what I was thinking, but it was almost comical to see both of their grinning faces nod at the same time.

"I suppose you two are going to tell me you knew what I was thinking just then," I said, still finding it hard to understand how that could be possible.

"Well now," Adrian replied in a matter-of-fact way, "it seems to me you've seen for yourself that thoughts can be very tangible things indeed, and that they can reveal their meanings from a distance."

That response led me to stare out to sea again and ponder the events of the past few minutes. Once more, I saw in my mind pictures of the little boy I had been when the lovely lady in the white habit had been my only friend. I remembered her rosy glow and the gentle, loving kindness she had embodied. Sitting beside me at that moment, as if no time at all had elapsed, was the same lovely lady, although she was wearing different clothes. At the time, the fact that she had not aged a day did not seem to have registered at all.

Adrian and Sister Diana waited patiently as I studied them together. For the first time I noticed a glow around Adrian that was similar to the glow I had always seen around Sister Diana, except that around him, deep violet colors were more pronounced and a beautiful turquoise band rippled from his midchest to his throat.

"The expression of love in various forms of communication such as oratory, poetry or literature yields the turquoise that now fascinates you, dearheart," Sister Diana explained, pinpointing my silent observation. "The colors have a language all their own and speak in exquisite hues and lovely tones with myriad variations. Once the language of color has been studied and mastered, it can be interpreted vividly and precisely, far more so than any manmade language of written words or symbols. As you begin to absorb the wonderful language yourself, you will soon begin also to hear its companion expression, sound, filling out the framework of color."

As soon as she finished speaking, I heard, very faintly at first, something that sounded like a choir. Soon I could hear soft yet unmistakable music of magnificent, angelic proportions blending with and emanating from the shimmering colors surrounding my two friends. The voices swelled in perfect harmony and swept like an ocean wave through my heart and soul. As the music grew, the glowing light surrounding my friends rippled and swirled like currents in a clear mountain stream eddying their way to a sea of peace. The sensation was both immensely elevating and deeply peaceful and I wished it would last forever.

"Never wish, my friend!" Adrian said firmly. "Never wish, but will, instead, and then focus on that will and you will always see your thoughts manifest before your expectant eyes in all their magnificent beauty and as permanently as your will commands."

That was too much for me. "I have seen, in my work and in my travels, determination and conviction as solid as steel, willpower you couldn't budge if you dropped a bomb on it, and yet the desired results were not always forthcoming or they fell well short of the intended objective. How can you say that willing something always makes it happen?"

Both Sister Diana and Adrian looked at me patiently and then at one another. Adrian nodded his head as if to indicate she should take over the lesson. "Consider the following simple metaphor, dearheart. Let us say a man boards a boat in the river of life and moves along its course. The boat is the thought; the objective, or destination, is the goal; and the boat's captain is the will."

I moved around in the sand so I could concentrate on her argument without distraction and eased into a wonderful sensation as I remembered how the child I was had listened to her explanations during the forest walks we always took.

"Now, as the boat and the captain move downstream they encounter many obstacles — rocks, fast currents, floating debris, other boats and all manner of potentially dangerous obstructions — impeding their course. Usually the obstacles can be successfully negotiated by the captain, that is, the will, thereby protecting the boat, or thought, from destruction."

As I focused on Sister Diana's metaphor, a memory from my past seeped into my mind. In my work as an architect designing the "big sandcastles" for people, as Sister Diana had so long ago prophesied, I had always seen in my mind's eye the object of my desire right from the beginning. I had known in advance that the unique approach I used in my work would lead me to encounter many obstacles along the way, yet by sheer force of will, I had always achieved the goal.

As a result, my many innovative designs had attracted worldwide acclaim, bringing me success, friends and influential international contacts. I considered all this as Sister Diana continued.

"Let us say, however, that the objective, the goal, is only a wish, lacking the life force that exists in the will. Then the boat is without a captain to guide it past the obstacles and eventually, inevitably, usually sooner than later, it flounders and goes down. The wish comes to naught. The result? The wisher gradually loses faith in his creative ideas, that is, his goals, and becomes part of the mass of people who are carried along like leaves in the wind of what they deem to be a cruel fate. That is tragic.

"What is even worse is those who use their will successfully but apply it to selfish goals," she said ominously, "for in their greedy accomplishments, they misuse their power and lose the opportunity to lead the less fortunate ones who do not understand this powerful law."

Sister Diana stopped speaking and Adrian picked up the thread of the conversation. "Let's look at another reason thoughts fail to manifest. Subtle fear-based doubts are often hidden from the thinker by pride, arrogance or even guilt. They wear many other clever masks as well and can remain camouflaged, deeply buried in the subconscious mind. Some fears represent lack of self-confidence, but more often they indicate lack of faith in others. Some fears reveal deep-seated feelings of unworthiness. That whisper of uncertainty causes the creative thinker's focus to blur. He begins to lose his stride toward his goal, and the frequency of his thoughts wobbles, causing the loss of momentum. The goal becomes harder and harder to hold on to, thus reducing the magnetism of his thought, which is essential for the thought to manifest.

"Eventually the imbalance causes the thinker to actually sabotage his own success. In many cases of failure, will is mistaken for stubbornness, an unwillingness or lack of awareness of the need for change. So what is the key ingredient?"

Before Adrian could finish, I jumped in. "Faith. That's what's necessary, isn't it? Faith!"

"Correct," Adrian replied, "but even with faith, the dark specter of doubt will rear its ugly head from time to time, so another ingredient must be added and that is persistence."

"So what you are saying is that if a person maintains persistent focused thought combined with faith, all thoughts, all goals will manifest, even though doubts creep in occasionally. Is that it?"

"Absolutely correct, my friend. And one thing more: it works for good and evil!" Adrian emphasized his statement with a serious frown.

At that point, Sister Diana suggested we drop the subject for the time being and go for a swim. After an invigorating splash, the three of us sauntered slowly across the beach and headed inland to an overgrown, mossy footpath that led to a wooded area.

Just ahead was a range of hills rising to a mountain that took my breath away. Its beauty and grandeur were like nothing I had ever seen before. The path itself was beautiful to behold. Wild hibiscus bushes covered with flowers of violet, yellow and white lined the trail. Here and there, also growing wildly but in perfect harmony with each other, were lovely white gardenias and tiny white geraniums.

We approached the fringe of the forest, where coconut palms whispered quietly as they stood like sentries, swaying to and fro in the gentle breeze. We walked silently in the cool air. Sister Diana produced a loose-fitting pastel blue jacket out of nowhere, it seemed, and put it around my shoulders. She and Adrian wore similar jackets but theirs were violet. Soon, I willingly abandoned myself to the lush blend of floral colors and aromas that wrapped themselves around me like a cloak.

We meandered slowly into the luxuriant forest and watched as a cute little squirrel monkey scampered along the branches of a breadfruit tree. A fallen eucalyptus tree was covered with soggy sphagnum moss, lichens, liverworts, orange-brown fungi and yellow helmet mushrooms with dainty bell-shaped caps. In the past I would have just jumped over the log and grumbled that it was obstructing my path, but as Adrian pointed out the abundant life forms that were using the fallen giant as their host and home, I developed a new respect for the ancient tree.

We walked around dogwoods boasting showy white blossoms. A sea of lily-of-the-valley blanketed the ground beneath several giant Douglas fir trees. Brown and yellow tree frogs, usually hidden from the eye, were easily spotted chirping their incessant cry all around us. I had often heard tree frogs at night but never during the day.

"Expect the unexpected from now on, dearheart," Sister Diana laughed.

"Oh, don't worry, nothing would surprise me now, not after what's already happened to me," I said.

"Don't be too sure of that, my friend," Adrian said. "The tip of the iceberg hides a large secret, as many a sailor has found out the hard way."

I nodded, accepting his suggestion. By then, I knew enough not to doubt him.

He pointed out a blanket of white-topped umbrella toadstools covering some moist leaves just off to the left of our path. To the right, a single golden shaft of sunlight pierced the dark green forest canopy. Two parrots flashed through the leaves in a blaze of blue, red and yellow, and I could hear the chatterings of small unseen animals in the underbrush. I had never experienced such serenity and splendor.

"It was always there, dearheart," Sister Diana chided, "you just never noticed it."

We walked on silently as I considered the truth of her words. How many wonders had I missed seeing even though they had been right under my nose? I resolved to change all that when I got back. But back from where? I had no real idea of where I was or why I was there. And with a little pondering on the subject I realized I was beginning not to care if I ever got back. I had never felt so secure, so peaceful and so wrapped in love as I did then. So why would I want to leave?

"Heaven is what you think it is, my friend, what you believe it is. To one person Heaven could be an eternity of singing hymns in some angelic kingdom in the clouds, while to another it could be eons spent fishing on a placid lake, without insects and with plenty of beer."

I had become accustomed to their comings and goings through my thoughts and was comfortable with such personal association because of my deep trust in them. They always gave me space to reflect on their words until I was ready to answer or to question them further. There was never a hint of condescension or superiority, and the greatest care and compassion were given to even the least delicate subject to ensure that I remained in a calm and positive state of mind.

Eventually, the three of us reached a wide ridge. Rounding a stand of magnificent cedar trees nestled amongst a grouping of huge boulders, we found a cheerfully warbling waterfall chiseled into the rocky mountainside among giant mountain ashes, ancient redwoods and towering eucalyptus trees. The waterfall descended about thirty feet into a small pool, then cascaded down several hundred feet into a larger pool beside the plateau below, spraying rainbow-colored mists along the rocky wall on its way.

Flowers of startling beauty and color peeked from between rocks and surrounded bushes. Stalks of violet-streaked white lilies leaned against the rocky face. Peacock-blue petals with orange sepals were surrounded by dark green, swordlike leaves that speared their way toward the sky.

I stood in silent rapture as Sister Diana pointed out the plants and flowers, naming each one as though they were friends, just as she had done so many years before. However, I could not remember ever having seen anything so abundantly beautiful during my forest walks with her as a child. Nor had I ever before experienced a setting more sensuous, more inviting or more tranquil. A collage of aromas intoxicated my senses and sent my mind into raptures. An ever deepening sense of peace and security suffused my entire being. I felt like a quietly purring pussycat comfortably sleeping beside a crackling fire.

"You are as secure as you believe in your heart you are," Sister Diana remarked casually as she and Adrian sat down on a large slab of granite near the pool's edge. They unloosed their sandals and let their feet dangle in the cool crystalline water while the gentle spray from the waterfall above sparkled on their faces. They looked like two happy-go-lucky children without a care in the world.

But my idyllic peacefulness was disturbed by an uncomfortable thought: Was I still in the world?

Sister Diana compassionately smiled with understanding as Adrian prepared to answer the unasked question that had been troubling me. Despite the glorious surroundings and the company of my wonderful friends, a gnawing desire to know the truth persisted subtly beneath the surface of my thoughts. And always, there was a growing sense of urgency. Even though we seemed to have unlimited time on our hands, I felt increasingly anxious to move on to something that was of profound importance.

"You have almost figured it out for yourself, dear friend, as we knew you would if given enough time." He smiled affectionately as I waited for the terrible words that I expected would confirm my fate. "You are in the world of thought, my brother, a world where what you think manifests as quickly as it is pictured in the mind. It is a world in which, as I have said before, Heaven is what you think it is. Peace is an instant reality that needs no thought except to let go of the thoughts that are less friendly.

"You are between worlds, sandwiched between the physical world as you know it and the infinite. It is here, Jonathan, that you will discover your destiny, the destiny that our Sister here first prepared you for as a lonely little orphaned boy. It is the destiny you have worked toward and studied for a lifetime to prepare yourself for, although you knew it not. And we, your true and loving friends, are here to take you over the remaining bridges to full awareness of what awaits you."

Although I had suspected I was no longer in the world of the living, Adrian's words told me that the situation was far stranger than I could have imagined. What could he have meant when he said that I had studied and worked for this destiny? If I was dead, I was dead and that was that, wasn't it? I was in an idyllic mountain paradise with my wonderful friends. Why did my past matter? And why had Adrian said I would find my destiny? What destiny?

As these thoughts galloped through my mind, I could faintly hear the echo of Sister Diana's last words to a sobbing little boy:

"My little angel, someday we shall once again sit on a beach together like this and walk and talk, and I will help to lead you to your destiny."

7

THE VISION

"BUT AM I DEAD? PLEASE, I MUST KNOW. AM I DEAD?" I PLEADED with my companions to tell me, as all the anxiety of my withheld emotions began to pour out. They looked on with patience and compassion but retained their calm composure. As they moved closer to me the beautiful colors and intoxicating aromas of their energy fields engulfed me in a wave of peacefulness, which allowed me to relax. I sank gently down onto a flat boulder.

As soon as I closed my eyes I again experienced the vision I had had on the aircraft before meeting Adrian. I saw myself riding the great wave of brilliant translucent light, but the sunlike disk seemed to be much closer, and this time I observed that two of the triangular pieces were illuminated in brilliant "living" yellow. The others remained grayish.

The vision lasted only a moment. Then Sister Diana instructed me to open my eyes and peer steadily into the still mountain pool beside the boulder on which I was sitting. Slowly my gaze grew more focused. The shimmering reflection of swaying eucalyptus branches disappeared from the water's surface and was replaced by a snow-covered mountaintop seen from a considerable elevation.

As the scene became clearer, I saw, trudging through the snow about halfway up the side of the mountain, a band of perhaps twenty travelers. They cautiously snaked their way up the side of the peak carrying ropes, knapsacks, stretchers and powerful hand-held searchlights. Passing a cluster of boulders they rounded a bend and came upon a metal object protruding fifteen feet out of a snow bank. It was the tailfin of an aircraft.

My heart jumped into my throat. I withheld a gasp and continued to watch, transfixed, as the ominous scene unfolded. The rescuers plodded past the tailfin and soon came upon many more pieces of the wreckage. Baggage, food trays, pieces of landing gear and jagged metal fuselage parts were scattered everywhere along with bodies and parts of bodies lying there lifelessly in ugly contrast to the pristine snow.

The fires had long since burned themselves out, leaving only the charred remains of metal and the once living flesh-and-blood remains of human beings.

Although the scene was grisly, except for an initial shock I observed it with complete dispassion. Then one of the rescuers crunched through the encrusted snow toward an unusual object projecting from a snowdrift. It was a bright blue flight bag hanging grotesquely by its strap from a frozen hand sticking out of the snow. My vision zoomed in more closely on the macabre setting and I noticed a delicate green jade stone set in gold that adorned the ring finger of the icy hand.

The vision faded and I took a deep breath, sighed and let my shoulders relax. My head dropped to my chest and as it did, my eyes fell upon the beautiful jade ring I had acquired in the Orient.

Although I felt profound relief that finally, I knew the truth, I was exhausted and needed to release the great strain of the uncertainty I had been holding in my mind and body. Sister Diana and Adrian helped me to my feet and led me to the base of a majestic pine tree, where I laid down my weary body, resting my head on a delicate cushion of pine needles. I took a deep breath of the heady aroma of flowers and pine needles and drifted into peaceful oblivion.

I had no way of knowing how long I had been asleep, but when I awoke I was no longer lying on my pine needle bed in paradise, and Sister Diana and Adrian were nowhere to be seen.

Instead, I was sitting on a high stool on the stage of a domed stadium. Filled, it would easily accommodate seventy thousand people. Lighting and sound technicians bustled about arranging the stage for some important function while maintenance people cleaned rubbish from aisles and stairways. The sound system was tested and tested again until the technicians were satisfied. The lights were adjusted and focused from several points onto a single location where stagehands were busy setting up an odd podium that had a wide ramp rising up to the center of it from the back.

I began to sense that my presence was not known to anyone and that was confirmed when two men carrying a long ladder approached me. Before I could get out of the way, the ladder passed directly through my body without my feeling the slightest sensation except the thrill of the experience. In fact, it made me slightly giddy and I laughed nervously to myself.

The entire scene meant nothing to me and I passed it off as the equivalent of a dream, albeit a vivid one, which meant I must still be sleeping peacefully under the pine tree. In any case, the meaning eluded me, although I was beginning to enjoy the strange sense of power it gave me. That was the last thing I recalled before the room faded and I lost consciousness.

When my eyes opened, I was indeed lying on my bed of pine needles, and Adrian was leaning over me smiling tenderly, like a loving parent. Nothing was said as he offered his hand to help me up. I got to my feet feeling wonderfully refreshed, invigorated and youthful.

"Well, my dear brother, how are you feeling now?" Adrian asked.

"I feel twenty years old and full of energy. I guess I'm a bit sad, but I'm ready, I think, for whatever lies ahead."

"Excellent! We have waited much longer than you might imagine to hear you say that, my friend," Adrian responded jubilantly. "Soon, much of your confusion will fade in the clarity of a new awakening." He walked over to the pool's edge and I followed. We sat down on a flat rock and gazed at the sublime beauty that surrounded us, our hearts filled with joy.

At the base of the pine tree under which I had slept Sister Diana was pensively scratching letters into a small smooth rock with a sharp object. The words were

> Jonathan King
> The Millennium Tablets
> Preparation

8

LOVE ATTRACTS

A MOMENT LATER SISTER DIANA JOINED THE TWO OF US AND TOOK my hand lovingly. I looked into her eyes and affectionately tightened my grip. She had an earnest expression on her lovely face that caused me to straighten up and pay close attention to what she said.

"Remember, dearheart, when I first arrived I said I thought you had put me on the back shelf of your mind in favor of things you felt were more important?"

I nodded and was about to deny it when she squeezed my hand lightly and shook her head with an understanding look to indicate all was forgiven.

"When I left you on the beach as a little boy we agreed to play a game, remember? A very special game of hide-and-go-find. You were very excited to play but preferred I not hide so well. Over the years that followed, I came to you many, many times but your vision had not grown enough to see through my disguises. Soon, new friends and your penchant for design filled the lonely spaces I once had shared with you, and my image began to fade from your thoughts. The painful abuse you endured from the other little children in the orphanage taught you not to speak about my visits, and eventually the grown-up world convinced you that a being such as I existed only in fairy tales.

"The years brought you into manhood and your recollection of me became a faded memory of some happy dreams that occurred during the nightmare years after your parents died, the creative imaginings of a frightened and lonely little boy playing make-believe."

I sighed and nodded my head. "I am so happy, Sister Diana, that the dream was not imaginary after all."

She smiled lovingly and continued. "As you grew up, your childhood love of building sandcastles led you to the study of architecture. Your aunt and uncle traveled a great deal and you had wonderful opportunities to see many of the beautiful structures of the world. Your mind embraced the various systems, concepts and interpretations of shape and form and you achieved an understanding of the cultures that had created the particular styles. Through that insatiable desire to absorb all the diversities of shape and form grew a versatile, pliable mind that we could mold."

I lifted my eyebrows at that revelation and became more interested in where Sister Diana was going with her biography.

"You experienced many satisfying moments designing your buildings once you had graduated from architecture school and, as we had hoped, your childhood tendency to withdraw into yourself evolved creatively and matured into an inner focus, a concentration that allowed us to feed your hungry mind lofty ideas."

Something in these words hit a soft spot within my ego and I childishly blurted out, "Are you trying to tell me that all the success I earned was actually planted in my mind, programmed by you two?"

Sister Diana and Adrian roared with laughter. "You should see the color of your thoughts at this moment, dearheart."

Adrian put his hand on the back of my head and gently pushed it forward so I could see my reflection in the water. I gasped in shock at the blazing inferno that appeared to engulf my body. Scarlet reds and muddy oranges flashed and flamed, while dirty brown stringy ribbons strangled my midsection and forehead. My stomach was in a knot and my head felt as though it were squashed in a vise.

My two laughing friends put their arms around my waist from either side and soon I began to calm down and breath evenly. As I relaxed, a tiny smile broke through the tense muscles of my face and finally, I joined in their laughter, seeing how foolish I had been.

"You see, my impulsive friend, your thoughts do have substance. If they are held in the mind long enough, they eventually crystallize in the material world. The problem is that most people cannot see them as you just have. Otherwise, they would think twice before allowing most of their thoughts to be expressed. A wise man once said, 'Circumstance does not make the man; it reveals him to himself.'"

Then Sister Diana added another thought. "On the other hand, if people could see their thoughts they would soon learn to separate the beautiful from the dark. Then they could focus their attention on building those thoughts that create peace and harmony in their lives. Until now, the vast majority of people, failing to understand this part of the law of creation, have focused on those things that produce immediate results, things which are often transient in nature and soon bring disappointment."

Adrian nodded in agreement.

"Wait a minute!" I interjected. "Are you saying that man can create his own reality? All of it? That there is no such thing as fate?"

"Well, no, not exactly," Adrian answered. "There are definite boundaries around each person's destiny. Compare it to a river. It can be wide or narrow as you swim through life, but within the boundaries of its banks, all things are possible to the swimmer."

"That's right, Jonathan," Sister Diana added enthusiastically. "Whether it is the power of selfless leadership or the force flowing through healing hands, so much is available to all of humanity through the correct use of creative imagination. However, the opposite is often what people receive, even though the same creative power is used, in that case used incorrectly. People literally create their own realities from minute to minute. When that great truth is fully realized, people can shift their attention to thoughts that create beauty, peace and love in their lives."

"As you will remember, we explained that consistent, focused thoughts combined with faith are required in order for the thoughts to manifest in the material world," Adrian continued. "This is fortunate, because if all his peoples' thoughts manifested, they would be in hot water most of the time."

I quickly agreed, with a grim smile.

"Many of these lifeless thoughts, as you might call them, lack the necessary power to come to fruition because of the illusion people have that they are limited, an illusion that has been planted in young minds down through the ages. But humans are not limited. This becomes more and more clear to people as they learn the true power of love."

While I certainly appreciated the value of love, I failed to see what Adrian was getting at, as he could tell from the expression on my face.

He smiled knowingly and continued. "Love, I am certain you will agree, is a binding force. It has therefore magnetic, cohesive properties. In other words, it draws things together. For example, all vegetation is drawn to the life-giving qualities of the sun, just as men and women are drawn to that portion of love in others that is missing in themselves. In fact, all life responds to the creative, life-giving properties of love. The plant promptly responds to the so-called green thumb of the one who loves his garden; animals react instantly to love and return it immediately. Only humans resist love, weighed down as they are by the ego's sense of limitation and the fear it generates in their hearts."

A thought occurred to me and I wanted to clear it up before my friends continued with their explanation. "Over the years I have designed entirely unique communities. Often I met with what at first seemed like insurmountable obstacles, yet eventually the solutions always came to me. Sometimes I would wake up with the answer fully developed in my mind. I once read that Mozart often heard an entire symphony go through his head in a moment. He was later able to write it down at his leisure, without having to make a single correction. While I don't compare myself to Mozart, I think my experiences were something like that.

"Other times the key to a tricky problem would come to me in the shower or maybe while sitting in traffic. And once, an incredibly difficult problem was solved while I was on an aircraft in a holding pattern above Chicago. Those moments of inspiration seemed to happen most often when my mind was occupied with something totally unrelated to the problem itself."

I got to my feet and began pacing back and forth, becoming more and more animated as a mist began to clear from my mind. "Each time those revelations came to me I knew the puzzle was complete. The experience was almost blissful."

By then I was nearly shaking. I looked over at Sister Diana and felt a shiver go up my spine. My face must have been radiant, to judge by the serene look in her eyes.

"You were there, weren't you?" I asked in a hushed tone. "It was you who gave me the answers, wasn't it?"

Sister Diana rose and tenderly embraced me. As we parted, she said, "You are almost there, dear Jonathan. Because of the strong binding tie of love between us I was able to provide a link through which the highest ideal or, as you would call it, solution, could penetrate your conscious mind. It was you who opened the channel with your consistent, focused concentration on your objective. The deep bond of love between us opened the final door."

Her face beamed with love until the light encompassed all three of us and the rosy glow that always surrounded her expanded to several times its normal size.

Then Adrian added, "Sister Diana herself did not actually give you the solutions; she was the catalyst. Once you had done the necessary groundwork she was permitted to open the doors that until then had remained shut to you. The key to that opening, as we have said, was love. Most people would call it passion, and by that I mean a deep desire to achieve your objective, combined with love. Your consistent, focused will, combined with your faith in yourself, which grew with each successive triumph, led to the final door that was opened by your passion."

I became silent for a moment, considering their words. "Let me see if I understand. A consistent, concentrated focus on an objective, together with passion, creates some kind of link with the power to manifest that objective. Is that it?"

"Correct!" Adrian and Sister Diana shouted in unison. Then Sister Diana added a footnote to my summary. "And the keynote to the process is the strength of your passion for the ideal. Or you could call it a burning desire combined with love. From the greatest to the smallest things in life, what you deeply love you attract to yourself."

I breathed a sigh of contentment as the concept's clear simplicity sank into my mind. Then Adrian, who had been staring into the mountain pool as Sister Diana was speaking, turned slowly toward me and spoke in a somber tone. "Unfortunately, my brother, this great power of manifestation works for both good and evil. As a result, much of what humankind has created throughout history has been based on selfish motives and has yielded great pain and suffering for all. Aiming for a higher purpose and thereby overcoming the temptation to misuse this enormous power is the great challenge facing humankind as the end of the millennium approaches. It is the destiny of the lightbearers of the world to show the way toward this manner of thinking and acting through the wisdom contained in the Millennium Tablets."

9

INTUITION, FREE WILL AND ILLUSION

I WANTED TO ASK WHAT THEY MEANT BY "THE WISDOM OF THE Millennium Tablets" but at that point Sister Diana and Adrian closed their eyes and fell silent. I politely withdrew, knowing they would explain it to me when they were ready to do so, and returned to my bed of pine needles to think things through.

I lay down feeling very peaceful and inspired after our discussion. I breathed deeply of the beautiful fragrances that surrounded me and gazed thoughtfully at the patches of cloudless blue sky visible through the spreading branches of the pine tree above me. As I relaxed more fully, a strangely sublime meditative state came over me, and I became aware of a sensation of weightlessness. My mind was clear and focused and I felt potently alive, more alive than I remembered ever having felt, even during my most intense design work.

Suddenly the weightless sensation gave way to one of gentle upward movement. A moment later I saw the lowest branches of the tree above me close in upon me. I surprised myself by remaining perfectly calm, not a small accomplishment under the circumstances.

When I reached the lowest branches I fully expected them to halt my momentum, but to my delight and amazement they simply passed straight through my body as if I were made of thin air. Branch after branch seemed to fall through my body as I ascended higher and higher. It was an indescribable feeling that I experienced not physically but emotionally and mentally. I was so captivated by the event that although I was exhilarated, my emotions remained totally calm.

At the summit of the evergreen my body came to a full stop and straightened itself into an upright position. The panorama was truly magnificent. I gazed out over a rolling turquoise sea far below the celestial garden. Tiny whitecaps rhythmically danced, and the sandy beach ribboned along in unbroken harmony with the sea. Towering above me was the unyielding face of the mountain's upper reaches which rose rigidly to a snow-covered peak. Perched there triumphantly, with a commanding grandeur rivaling that of the mountain on which she sat, was a solitary peregrine falcon, reconnoitering her heavenly kingdom with majesty. She clutched something in one of her powerful talons. The elegant bird was curiously familiar and I felt strangely drawn to her.

Then my gaze descended slowly through an opening among the evergreen branches and I saw my friends still silently meditating on their granite bench. My eyes moved to my pine needle bed. Somehow, I was not surprised to see my stationary body still lying there resting peacefully, hands clasped behind its head. Nevertheless, it was definitely an eerie feeling to be separated from my body, and the tingling thought of it sent shock waves rippling through my floating form.

Suddenly, I felt like a speeding automobile traveling over a bumpy road. Instantly, I was back in my reclining body, and sporadic aftershocks continued to quake through me as I opened my eyes. Directly in front of me I found my two friends, grinning.

"I don't see anything particularly funny about it!" Adrian helped me to my feet. "One minute I'm floating among the treetops like Superman and the next thing I know, the mountain caves in on me."

Adrian and Sister Diana giggled like two children as I persisted in my grumbling. They led me back to where they had been sitting at the pool's edge, and we sat down with me in the middle. I was not really perturbed, so I stopped complaining and said, "I've read many stories about out-of-body experiences. They often document people who have been on operating tables when their hearts have stopped beating. I think those kinds of out-of-body experiences are called near-death experiences. Sometimes the articles described violent car crashes or other accidents. Apparently there are thousands of well-documented cases of near-death experiences, and almost all the victims report nearly identical recollections of what happened while they were apparently dead."

My friends listened patiently, as loving parents would with children as they explained any activity that was new and exciting to them.

"Quite frankly, I dismissed the stories for that very reason. They were all so similar. You know, long tunnels, bright lights, beautiful angelic figures or loving friends and relatives who had passed away coming to greet them and telling them to go back because it wasn't their time yet. I thought it was strictly science fiction and fodder for gullible minds. But now I don't know what to think."

I hesitated for a moment to reflect, watching the sun dance on the surface of the mountain pool. The cool air was invigorating and my senses felt sharper than ever. I could hear playful rustling nearby in the oleander shrubs as a red squirrel chased a black one. My own out-of-body experience hadn't been a near-death experience and was no match for the ones I had read about, but how could I deny the existence of such a thing any longer?

"If those stories were true, then how come I didn't see any tunnels or lights or angels? All I saw was the scenery here, beautiful though it is, and, oh yes, the most magnificent falcon I've ever seen."

Adrian looked at Sister Diana who smiled and nodded to him.

"The objective of the experience and the guidance connected to it vary. Therefore, circumstances have to vary as well. As I have already pointed out, the greatest enemy humankind has to face today is fear — fear of failure, fear of loss and, the worst enemy of all, fear of death. It is that stark terror of nonexistence that most people fear the most. They wonder what comes after physical death, if anything."

I nodded in agreement.

"The Universal Intelligence behind all that exists allows humans the incredible legacy of free will, the freedom to choose their own paths of development. Although there are many restrictions and barriers along the path of what you have called fate, humans have free will and may choose within the boundaries of their fate."

Adrian hesitated, then picked up a small pointed stone. With it he drew two parallel lines on the smooth rock and then drew a stick figure between them. "Once again, let's use our metaphor about the river of life. We will say that this person is a swimmer and the river represents his lifetime. Before he begins his journey through the school of life, he is totally conscious of his destination which is complete, conscious reunion with the ocean — that is, Universal Intelligence, or Spirit. Once he begins his pilgrimage to his true home in the ocean, he encounters many options among which he must choose. Sometimes the river's water will be rough and choppy while at other times it will be calm, placid and peaceful. The river will be narrow in some places and wide in others, deep in some spots and shallow in others. In fact, he may find it so shallow and peaceful in some places that he can stand still and not move down the river at all. That could be a wonderful, rejuvenating interlude but could be a nasty trap if indulged in for too long, for life is ever-changing movement and will tolerate no lethargy. The penalty is stagnation and death.

"Now it is important to understand that the swimmer cannot go beyond the boundaries of the river's banks. These, as we have discussed, are the preset limits of his life's fate when he begins his return to the ocean. He does, however, have many choices along the way. He can flow with the current or swim against it. He can rest in the shallows from time to time or get stuck there, mired in the quicksands of indifference, failing to reach his objective. His judgment — the choices he makes — will speed his swim home, slow it down or prevent it from occurring altogether.

"The courageous swimmer will forge ahead, pushing past the debris and distractions in his way. That is, he will swim past the illusion of limitation, the illusion of immovable objects and the distraction of transient temptations that threaten to prolong his journey to the ocean, to Spirit. As the swimmer learns to face and conquer these illusions, he strengthens his confidence and his resolve to reach his destination at any cost. He develops a no-matter-what attitude. In other words, as he persists in moving toward his objective with his focused concentration, it becomes an increasingly strong desire, or passion."

As Adrian spoke, I again had a vision of an enormous tidal wave of light. Not only did I view the great wave from the top but somehow, simultaneously, from a distance. It was carrying me forward at an incredible speed, and once again the sunlike disk was in front of me, but now it was much closer. The two brilliant gold, triangular pieces were glowing even more brightly than before, and I could make out lettering on the two pieces. The lettering on the first was the same as on my little yellow stone amulet: MT-I. The second one read MT-II. In the middle of the disk within a circle it said 144,000. And again I heard the child's voice. It was saying, "the Millennium Tablets."

I was near the front of the wave and this time there were others with me. A few older people were behind me but most of the people were much younger than I, the majority being children, and the strange thing was that everyone appeared to be delighted and not the least bit frightened. I was both observing and living in the slightly scary scene, and yet I could still clearly hear Adrian speaking. The vision wasn't distracting me at all.

"It is in the nature of the river to present to the swimmer opportunities that would increase his capacity to reach his destination quickly. These opportunities often come in the form of apparent obstructions, but they are never so formidable that the swimmer can't handle them. I'm certain you will agree that many people who have faced incredible hardships or challenges in life have felt the obstructions were beyond their ability to surmount; often, that mistaken attitude led them to give up without really trying, thereby missing the blessing of the guidance intended by the difficulty.

"You see, the river of life and the ocean are already connected. And the ocean, through the river's intimate contact with the swimmer, constantly provides him with the easiest way to return to itself. This guidance is called intuition and is available to all of humanity all of the time. The challenge is to listen to that guidance. Usually the swimmer requires many nudges in the right direction by the ocean's guidance, by his intuition and through many failures due to his indifference to that guidance before he begins first to listen to it and then to obey it. That moment of acceptance is a marvelous turning point for the swimmer, for then all of life begins to bend in his favor to help him to return to his home in the ocean of Spirit."

As Adrian finished his dissertation, Sister Diana looked me straight in the eyes. While I'd never known her eyes to be without great gentleness, I had begun to see within those lovely eyes the infinite depth and power of the universe, and whenever they caught mine, they held me totally captive.

"Herein lies the dark undercurrent of humankind's long suffering. Fear and the sinister illusion it creates have caused the swimmer to forget his destination is the ocean of Spirit. The result has been doubt, despair and hopelessness. A wise man once said, 'The ocean is not diminished by the missing drop of water but the drop of water certainly misses the power of the ocean.'"

Suddenly a wonderful thought occurred to me. "These out-of-body occurrences — could they be part of a grand design to give hope to a world steeped in the hideous illusion that death is a final curtain instead of the glorious transition into a much higher expression of reality that it really seems to be? Could it be that the people who have gone through these experiences were not ever meant to die but that the episodes were somehow staged to show them a fragment of the real life they would return to one day? And could it be that they were supposed to take that information back to the world in sufficient numbers and with enough credibility that only the most hardened skeptics would fail to believe?"

"No, dearheart," Sister Anne replied, "these experiences are not staged. Rather, they are simply utilized as the opportunities present themselves. Remember, humans have free will, and Universal Intelligence never interferes with that gift. The ocean of Spirit makes use of every opportunity to awaken the semiconscious, weary swimmer who has often replaced hope and awareness with fear and illusion. And the lessons that usually come in the form of obstacles and challenges take many different disguises."

"This all makes a great deal of sense to me now, but there is something nagging me about my own experience. Since I am apparently no longer in a physical body, how then was it possible for me to leave whatever body I now possess?"

Sister Diana smiled knowingly, as she often did. She took my hand in hers and held it up in front of my eyes. "What makes you think you have only one body?"

With a frown, I looked at the hand I possessed. It looked exactly as it had always looked. She gave me back my hand and continued.

"When you first saw me when you were a child in your lonely little room and again on the beach near your aunt and uncle's home, did I appear different from the way I look now?"

I considered the question carefully and then replied, "Other than your style of dress, I see little change except that the glow that surrounds you seems more vivid than I remember it to have been."

"And?"

"The fragrance. The lovely aroma. When I was a small boy, I never noticed it, but now it's unmistakable, even from a distance."

"Exactly! Two important things have occurred. First, many of the illusions and distractions that affected your physical senses have fallen away, so you observe more easily what has always been present.

"Second, and more specific to your question, there are a great many levels of consciousness. Your scientists have known for years that even the individual cells of a physical organism have a unique consciousness all their own, and that consciousness responds directly to a person's thoughts. A gloomy, negative, pessimistic attitude will register almost immediately on the face and soon afterwards throughout the entire body, as the immune system begins to become sluggish. I am sure you will agree it is not a difficult matter at all to read much of an elderly person's lifetime attitude by looking at the lines and expression on his or her face.

"Each and every level of thought, whether it is emotional, mental, intuitive or higher, manifests on increasingly finer planes, or levels, of existence. Each possesses a distinctive cloak, or vehicle, of its own and all interpenetrate one another just as they do in your worldly activities.

"For example, the falcon you identified with was . . . "

"An aspect of myself in a form that metaphorically represented a more elevated attitude," I exclaimed excitedly.

"I think he's got it!" Adrian said with a sophisticated British accent.

Peals of our laughter echoed throughout the valley below. As I tilted my head back, I happened to notice that the upper branches of the redwood on the opposite side of the pool had begun to fade.

As I bent forward, rubbed my eyes and looked again, I saw, directly in front of me, crowds of people pouring into the giant stadium I had witnessed before. Great expectation shone on their faces. Unfamiliar yet beautifully inspirational sounds filled the space. I felt my heart swelling with excitement as I began picking up the rising spirit of the impending event.

"What could this wonderful scene mean?" I wondered, and yet somehow, I felt intimately involved in it.

10

THE WORK OF THE LIGHTBEARERS

I WAS STILL DEEPLY ABSORBED IN THE POWERFUL VISION WHEN Adrian broke in. He spoke softly, gently nudging my focus back to the mountain sanctuary. "I feel we are being ignored, Sister Diana."

"Then we must fold our tents and look elsewhere for companionship that treats us with more respect," she said with an impish grin.

The two were quietly giggling as I gradually eased back into my normal senses. One moment I was listening to my friends speaking over the auditorium sound system, and the next thing I knew, I had returned to my place beside them. I watched their amused expression, but my mind was drawn back to the fascinating images I had just seen. The fact that the scene had evolved since my first view of it made it all the more intriguing. As captivating and beautiful as it was, it was also very disturbing.

For some reason that had so far escaped me, I had not yet felt the need to share the strange vision with my friends. Based on their grasp of my thoughts so far, I was very sure they knew what I was experiencing anyway, and I suspected that they had a very specific purpose for the guidance they were giving me. So I elected to just wait for them to reveal what that purpose was when they were ready.

"Your inner perception is quickly sharpening, dearheart," Sister Diana offered with encouragement.

"And I can assure you, my friend, you will need it," Adrian added in a serious tone.

I sensed that it would be a good time to ask a question that had been on mind since before my little float above the treetops. "Adrian, you mentioned something to the effect that it is the responsibility of the lightbearers to show the way to a new kind of thinking. Who are these lightbearers and how do they do that?"

Adrian's smile was full of warmth and understanding. He put his arm affectionately around my shoulder and said, "You have arrived at the very threshold of the place we have been preparing you to enter throughout your life, dear friend, and we are delighted to see you are almost ready."

"How do you know I am ready? All I did was ask who the lightbearers are," I said with a puzzled expression.

"My friend, you wear your heart on your sleeve in the most literal sense. In this world, 'you know even as you are known.' As we have explained to you, the most minute change of mind, any opening in the fabric of understanding, any heartfelt desire — all register in the cloaks we wear around us.

"You need only to learn how to observe the colors and read them closely. Armed with such understanding, you can quickly know the true pattern of a being's thoughts and the feelings behind them."

My eyes lit up as I realized the incredible possibilities such power offered. "Would it not then be impossible to utter a lie or to mask a dark thought? It would immediately be exposed to all who could read the meaning of the cloaks."

"As our brother Adrian has said, dearheart, 'You know even as you are known,'" Sister Diana confirmed.

"Wow! That would eliminate all sorts of pride and deceit. People would have to get on with their lives without false coverings, game playing and manipulation."

Adrian broke out in a broad grin, obviously pleased at my growing understanding of the truths I was being shown.

"The lightbearer must understand many things if he or she is to set the example of leadership that is so critically required in the world at this juncture, which is the planet's most important turning point since its beginning."

I was still intoxicated by my discovery of the power inherent in the ability to read colors, when a staggering thought instantly sobered me up. "Lightbearer? Understanding? What are you two saying?" I asked nervously. "Do you guys mean to say — that is, are you trying to tell me or show me, that . . . that . . . somehow I am to be a lightbearer?"

Sister Diana placed her hand on top of my head and repeated the words she had said to me so long ago. "My little angel, someday we shall once again sit on a beach together like this and walk and talk, and I will help to lead you to your destiny."

As she spoke, the glassy surface of the mountain pool reflected a stretch of white sandy beach where a small boy was lying with his head on the lap of a beautiful lady dressed in a pure white nun's habit and surrounded by a heavenly rosy glow. Tears filled my eyes as the treasured scene was replayed for me. I sadly relived the departure of my beloved Sister Diana soon after she had spoken those prophetic words.

I breathed deeply as the water resumed its reflection of our peaceful sanctuary. I looked at my friends. They sat placidly amid the fragrance of the lush green pines and eucalyptus trees. A majestic bird circled in the cloudless sky, spiraling lower and lower and finally landing on top of a sharp rock at the summit of the waterfall, just above the pool. It was the beautiful falcon I had seen earlier.

I had often seen images of such a bird in ancient Egyptian architecture, where it represented Horus. It was usually worn on the head by a pharaoh, and it symbolized the highest aspect of human consciousness.

The exquisite bird's riveting stare bore down upon me. The link between us was powerful, and something about the proud creature gave me a sense of unconquerable strength and confidence. The bird seemed to embody endurance, perseverance and the mastery of challenges.

Although I somehow felt a slight foreboding about the answer, I asked, "Do lightbearers work on the physical side as well as on this side?"

"We are privileged to work on both sides, as you saw Sister Diana do when you were a child," Adrian replied with humility. "However, at this critically important turning point in your planet's destiny there are still many who are totally unaware of their identity as lightbearers and of the great task before them. From this side, they are gently and silently led by their guides and guardians from the day of their entrance into the school of life."

"Guardians? School of life? Wait just a moment, please. Let's slow down for the beginner here," I quipped.

We laughed and Sister Diana offered a word of encouragement. "From early childhood right up until the accident that claimed your parents' lives, we saw you as a soul of great potential. That is why we encouraged you not to leave the school of life when that particular opportunity presented itself to you."

"Well, thank you very much for your faith in me, but I think you have accelerated the conversation again rather than slowing it down, haven't you?" I teased. "Now you're saying I had a choice, given to me by you two, of whether or not to live when my parents' car went over the cliff? Is that what I'm supposed to believe?" I had a look of skepticism on my face as I waited for their reply, but all they did was remain very quiet and let the information sink in.

Then I remembered the part about loved ones telling a person undergoing a near-death experience that it was not his time and that he needed to return. What I hadn't known was that each person could actually choose, under certain circumstances, to stay, whether it was his time or not. I reconsidered my outburst but was still confused.

"Okay, okay, I remember. We know as we are known. So why should you guys lie to me, right? What's the point? But wow, it's a lot to swallow. I mean a person having a choice about whether or not to die. Why give a choice to someone? Unless he just didn't feel like living anymore, wouldn't everyone choose to live if he were in an accident and had a choice? I just couldn't seem to get past my habitual pragmatism and reach deeper into the idea to find understanding. Adrian gently countered my misgivings with a question of his own.

"Since you have been here, my friend, would you not agree that your experience has been somewhat pleasant?"

I didn't need any time to think about that one and immediately responded, "Other than the first part, which was confusing and upsetting, it's easily the most peaceful and uplifting experience I've ever had."

"I'm sure you'll also agree that even the upset could have been far more traumatic had your mind and the minds of the other passengers on the plane not been blacked out during the moments just before the crash," Adrian added.

That comment opened a mental door for me.

"Of course!" The entire pattern of events, including the landing and all that had occurred afterwards, must have been intended to bring all the passengers gently to a realization of what had happened to them and to an understanding of the transition they were going through. "And presumably, all of them are going through the same stages of indoctrination into this side of life as I'm experiencing."

"Not quite the same, Jonathan," Sister Diana interjected. "Remember, you still have business to attend to on the physical side, while none of those particular souls do. They must busy themselves sifting through the lives they have just completed for the pearls of wisdom they will integrate into their souls. With the help of their guardians and guides, they must also face the many lost opportunities and the errors they made in thought, word and deed. In that way they will climb the rungs of the ladder to greater awareness and, eventually, to complete awakening."

Sister Diana waited patiently while I considered that for a moment. Then she continued. "Each soul is given the opportunity to review the recently completed life and take stock of what you might call the credits and debits that have been accumulated. Then they absorb the positive accomplishments that were of a permanent nature, such as services rendered to their fellow human beings. This process can take weeks or years of Earth time to finish, but once it is completed, the soul is given a choice of many new opportunities to serve, thereby continuing its climb toward total spiritual awareness.

"The process is without end. Once full awakening has been achieved, whether it takes place on Earth or in the higher planes of existence, then the real life begins. From then on true creative fulfillment occurs in total cooperation with Universal Intelligence, or Spirit.

"Although the process of awakening can indeed be completed on this side, it is the physical world with all its suffering, illusions and fears that is the best environment for this transition to occur quickly. That is because the very resistance caused by struggle forces a soul to grow.

"Consider the growth of a plant and how much of its life is spent in total darkness, struggling toward the light. And yet the result is a strong root system, a foundation able to sustain the beautiful leafy development once the light is reached.

"When guided by the wisdom of intuition, a person can accomplish phenomenal things in a few short years. Your history books are filled with the wonderful achievements made by souls who were tuned in. Whether they were consciously aware that they were is not important. The fact is that they had tapped into the creative impulses available to all humankind and obeyed their so-called hunches instead of their emotions or fallible human reason. That is what occurred throughout your life, Jonathan, and it is the very reason you are now on the threshold of a great opportunity to serve.

"Most awakened souls elect to continue working on this side where there is no conflict, no hatred, no greed and no death. How could those things exist when all that one could want is only a thought away? And as you are now aware, we cannot hide who we are or what we think."

Sister Diana closed her eyes and stopped speaking for a moment. Within seconds, before my startled eyes a plate of luscious tropical fruit appeared in her outstretched hands. She offered it to me and I took a large piece of pineapple.

Until then I had felt absolutely no hunger at all. I had not even thought of food. But the instant the delicious-looking food was in front of me, I suddenly became famished. I thanked her with a shaky voice and bit into the juicy fruit. The flavor of the pineapple was the most piquant and satisfying I had ever tasted and I nodded my approval as I ate.

Sister Diana calmly went on with her explanation as if nothing out of the ordinary had occurred. "A few elect to return to the Earth school to help their fellow humans on that level. Some who are more advanced go in and out of physical bodies as required or pass out of sight to a finer vibration, such as the one we now occupy, when it suits the purpose of their service.

"Of those who will return to Earth, many like you are being prepared at this critical turning point in human evolution into total awakening. The lightbearers cannot be pressed into service any too soon, for the energizing influence of this worldwide wake-up call is increasing by the minute and for those most soundly asleep the effect can be very uncomfortable. The work of the lightbearers is an immense aid during this transition in reducing the suffering of those souls who are in denial of the inevitable and wonderful changes now taking place. The souls who stay on this side remain just out of sight, working through receptive minds wherever they can be found, without regard to color, race, creed or Earthly status.

"The task is a formidable one since, at this point, most people are either totally unaware of the transition Earth is undergoing or simply do not believe in such things. Add to that the restrictions of finite human vision and the exercise of free will and it is easy to see why the positive seeds we plant in the minds of men and women often fail to take root and flourish."

While Sister Diana spoke, Adrian seemed to be watching my responses carefully. I am certain he knew how my pragmatic mind would react to the details of the expanded version of reality I was being taught. I had learned a lot since my first step into the broader understanding of life being explained to me by my friends. So far I had reacted with predictable resistance, gradually settling into a somewhat more open-minded and receptive attitude as these simple truths began to sink in. But could I face the task that seemed to lie before me? Was I capable of completing the assignment? While Sister Diana and Adrian's faith in me appeared great, I did have free will.

They knew I had a creative mind and although I had been unaware of it, I had long before linked up with the higher realms through the constant exercise of my intuition. My feet were firmly planted on the ground and yet I exercised a broad range of imaginative creativity in my work, which had brought me fame and fortune.

I was dogged in my determination to carry through any project I had set my mind to, without regard for obstacles. And I had an easygoing manner and was caring and compassionate about everyone I came into contact with, although I often failed to reveal that. A shield had surrounded me since the loss of my parents and not even the great success I had enjoyed in life had reduced its power over me.

Sister Diana and Adrian fully understood that the tools I had acquired and the level of awareness I was in the process of attaining could make me a most useful instrument for Spirit's purposes. Those tools still needed to be fleshed out through the final lifting of the veil of illusion. Once I comprehended at a higher level the causes behind effects and the permanence behind temporary shadows, my influence as a lightbearer during the critical changes about to occur could be enormous.

It was a question of timing, however, more than it was anything unique about me, for it has been said that God is no respecter of persons. Yes, I possessed the qualities for the job but the planet had produced many special souls during the long and arduous evolution of the human family. It had to be the timing.

The spiritual vibrations playing upon the planet were opening pathways that would rewrite the history books in a handful of years. That influence could catapult a soul who was prepared for service into a position of almost immeasurable power to influence men and women toward their true inheritance.

My friends knew the sacrifice that would be asked of me. Could I face it? That was one of the few questions they had been unable to answer since they had begun their task of molding me and guiding my growth when I was a child. Soon they would be ready to reveal the adventure that lay before me and the price I would have to pay to take my place among the privileged who would help humankind to move successfully into the new wave of light that was rapidly moving toward the Earth. Without my service and the service of the other lightbearers like me, many who could be saved would perish, and many who could be guided would endure immense suffering while resisting the strain of the changes that were quickly approaching.

11

MY FAITH IS TESTED

"MY FRIEND, IT IS TIME FOR US TO LEAVE THIS PLACID SETTING SO we can demonstrate the concepts we have shared with you so far," Adrian said. "It is important that you see the deep-rooted value of the concepts you are being taught and the effect they can have on your fellow humans should you accept the challenges ahead of you."

I took a deep breath and stood up. I paused for a moment and glanced up at the falcon, who had remained above us. Its eyes were steadily focused on me. Somehow, its presence felt comforting and protective, even though its piercing gaze gave me an uneasy feeling, a vague feeling of urgency.

Sister Diana and Adrian smiled kindly at me as if to indicate that a phase of their guidance had come to an end. The cap and gown and the diploma had been put away and the graduate was taking his first step toward higher attainment through service.

Adrian led the way as Sister Diana firmly clasped my hand in support and encouragement. As we ascended farther up the mountainside, my falcon friend spread its magnificent wings and soared down to the rocky platform we had just left behind. Beneath its powerful talons I saw the following words:

> Jonathan King
> The Millennium Tablets
> Understanding

✧   ✧   ✧

Although we climbed for about an hour, I felt no fatigue at all. The air became more and more rarefied and my senses more and more acute. It seemed as if the very essence of the evergreens' vitality filled my body, and the wildflowers' perfume grew in intensity with each upward step. I felt grandly inspired and able to tackle any challenge that might present itself to me.

My supportive friends could see the growing strength within me as the colors that surrounded me glowed brighter and brighter. They felt certain of my readiness but allowed no excessive confidence to divert their focus, for they knew the most difficult challenge was still ahead of me.

The path made a sudden sharp turn and we faced a smooth rock wall. There appeared to be no way to climb it without the proper equipment, and I felt certain we would have to end our ascent at that point.

Adrian read the finality of my conclusion. Such a reaction was typical of the limited thinking of most humans.

"I am surprised at you, my friend," Adrian began. "How many times have you faced a complex problem with apparently no direction to go but down and eventually solved it?"

Slightly embarrassed about my impulsive conclusion, I sheepishly replied, "I guess in pretty much every important project I was involved in."

"And what value would you put on the ideas we have shared with you thus far, my Doubting Thomas friend?" Adrian grinned.

"Infinitely valuable!" I replied without hesitation.

"At this point in our relationship and after all that we have shared with you, is it likely that we would lead you to an impasse without a specific purpose?" Adrian continued.

I considered that for a moment and then an exciting thought came to me.

"Each time I came to, faced and eventually conquered what

appeared to be an insoluble problem in my work, I became not just more confident, but somehow more capable of tuning into the source of solutions. I guess you would say I strengthened my intuitive link to Spirit."

"Precisely," Sister Diana interjected. "The very struggle to solve your various challenges without thought of quitting led you inevitably to letting go and letting the answer come to you."

"Yes, I remember now. I would struggle and struggle. After studying the problem from every angle possible I'd focus on it until my brain felt fried. Then finally, mentally fatigued and on the verge of abandoning hope, I would just let go and that is when answers would flood into my mind. And the answers were always right in front of my nose and ridiculously simple — to the extent that I often felt embarrassed that I hadn't seen them sooner."

"And what do you perceive as the greater purpose of the seemingly useless waste of energy in this process?" Adrian asked.

I reflected a moment, then answered, "Until we have the faith to simply let go and let Spirit take over, we must continually go through the process of, first, exhausting our ego-based search for answers, second, abandoning the finite borders of our limited minds and, third, finally allowing a higher intelligence to intervene on our behalf and fill the vacuum left when we let go of the harder method.

"Through our free will we can choose the frustrating route as long as we desire to until finally, when we are sufficiently frustrated, we release our grip on the problem and allow Spirit, through intuition, to provide us with solutions to all problems. The key, therefore, is humility and the faith to let go."

I finished my analysis with a deep sigh of satisfaction, happy to finally understand the process I'd used successfully for so many years. I sat down on a nearby rock as my falcon friend swooped up the face of the mountain inches from where I sat and perched on a jagged ledge thirty meters above the three of us.

Sister Diana waited politely for a minute to be certain I had finished, then strode over and put her hand on my shoulder. As I looked up at her, it appeared that the falcon was perched on her shoulder. She finished my analysis with a softly spoken conclusion. "And, dearheart, it matters not what realm of life one comes from, whether it is the palace of a king, the halls of learning or the ghettos of poverty and ignorance. The door to creativity will always open to those who ask with faith and humility and nothing will be impossible to the ones who do."

Adrian looked at me. "Well, Jonathan, now that we have established that nothing is impossible, what do you say about this apparent impasse we have reached?"

I studied my friend's expression for a moment and found no clue to a possible answer. I turned my head and did the same with Sister Diana. Still nothing, only warm glowing smiles and patient expressions, as if we had all the time in the world.

I suppose we do have all the time in the world, I mused, since we are apparently living in the infinite now, whatever that is. I shook my head in frustration but remained silent, trusting my friends' advice and returning my attention to the problem at hand. I focused all my attention on the blank rock wall ahead of us as if it were one of my apparently insurmountable design problems.

Eventually, I began to get very tired and my eyelids drooped slightly, partially blurring my vision. Then I distinctly heard a voice in my mind say, "Faith will remove the mountain."

At that moment, before my half-shut eyes, I glimpsed a fissure in the rock wall. Inspired, I stood up and moved to one side. From that new position the sun shone from directly behind my falcon friend's perch. The shadow it cast against the presumably flat rock surface was not even but broken at the fissure I had spotted a moment before.

My friends began to grin like children. Excited, I walked over to the fissure and saw a narrow passageway between two flat portions of the mountain's face. There was an optical illusion that made it look as though there were a solid wall when it was viewed from all but that one angle — the angle cast by the falcon's shadow.

I looked triumphantly at my friends. Adrian walked over to the opening and pointed to the fissure. "It is at this point that many who are struggling to grow give up: the point where illusion and reality meet. Most never even see the fissure in what looks like a blank wall. They simply accept what they deem to be the inevitability of their so-called fate. Only a few in history have struggled on past the rock face and are shown the fissure. Even then, many still lack sufficient faith to press on by focusing on the clue they have been given and find the opening in the wall. Only a few, like you, Jonathan, who have struggled and faced many obstacles, have developed sufficient faith and determination to hold on until the solution comes to them."

Adrian paused for a moment, then turned the corner and disappeared through the opening. Sister Diana headed in the same direction and as she approached the opening, she turned her head and said, "This is why all must build their faith by focusing on the tiniest of successes in life. Through a one-day-at-a-time, one-success-at-a-time process they finally construct the habit of faith in which reality and truth dwell."

Then she too disappeared through the opening as I stood looking at it. One moment later two heads popped out of the opening like grinning puppets in a Punch and Judy show. Together, they said, "Coming?"

That tickled my funny bone and I burst out laughing as I headed toward the opening, hearing the echo of their laughter fading into the distance as they pushed on ahead of me.

12

APPROACHING LIGHT

I ENTERED THE NARROW GAP BETWEEN THE BREAK IN THE ROCKS and squeezed around a tight corner. The turn was so awkward that I wondered how both my friends had gotten their heads around the corner without letting their bodies show. The space between the rock walls was very narrow and it became darker as I continued forward. I moved my hands along the walls to keep my bearings on the twisted path. I could hardly hear Sister Diana as she called out from a distance, "The doors of awareness do not eliminate life's obstacles, Jonathan, but they do increase our ability to deal with them."

Wonderful, I thought. I'm buried inside a rocky tomb while my friends philosophize from a distance.

A few minutes later, I was in complete darkness. My fingers touched what felt like a metal wall, and when I moved the palm of my hand across the surface my suspicions were confirmed. I pushed it slightly but it wouldn't give. However, it seemed to rattle the way a loosely hinged door might. I felt around in the darkness for a door knob and sure enough, I found one. Turning it, I pushed my body slowly against the weight of the door. It wouldn't budge. With my other hand I searched around the knob for some kind of locking mechanism and finally found a bolt. I tried to slide it open, but it remained stuck. From the other side of the door I could hear Adrian's voice telling me to hold on.

A moment later the bolt jolted to the side and as the door swung open, I saw Adrian standing there in his airline captain's uniform with a screwdriver in his hand.

"Sorry for the inconvenience, Mr. King. What a coincidence that both the light and the door lock in the lavatory broke at the same time. We'll have to have them fixed right away."

I looked around and realized I was stepping out of the confines of an aircraft restroom. The situation had all the appearances of a man's being rescued by a plane's captain, and part of my mind found it amusing. As I turned to take a look back into the lavatory, the lights flickered and came on.

Adrian gave me a big grin and said, "By now, Jonathan my friend, not much of anything should surprise you!"

I shook my head and chuckled. "Oh, it's not that I'm shocked or even surprised, it's just that it's a little difficult to get used to a whole new set of rules that say anything is possible."

"In reality, Jonathan, everything is possible — even in the physical world. If it were not for the deep-rooted convictions of most people that there are limitations in that world and that humans are somehow separate from Spirit, so-called supernatural phenomena would become natural, and daily miracles would be the norm."

I nodded my head in half-hearted agreement, still not completely able to accept his simple truths.

As usual, he caught my misgivings and added in a serious tone, "We understand your doubt. It is wise to have an open-minded skepticism when dealing with anything that is a dramatic departure from your normal experience, for there is much deceit in the material world.

"Now, my friend, let us attend to the business at hand. We have returned to the final hours of your flight to help you rise above your doubts."

Again I felt a childlike sense of anticipation as Adrian led me down the passageway toward the rear section of the aircraft. Sitting in the aisle seat of the last row was Sister Diana, dressed in the white nun's habit I had always seen her in when I was a child. Beside her by the window was a tall thin man of perhaps sixty-five years of age who appeared to be very frail. Something about him seemed familiar, and I looked at Adrian inquisitively.

"That is Leon Krasnansky, the internationally famous tenor," Adrian said, anticipating my question. "You have seen him in many televised concerts, and you might recall that he was the headline performer at the inauguration of the concert hall you designed in Europe."

"That's right!" I exclaimed. "I met him briefly at a cocktail party afterwards, but that was many years ago. He was much stronger and heavier then. I think that's why I didn't recognize him right away."

"He is dying of cancer and would have had only a few more months to live," Adrian explained.

A sharp pang passed through my heart. I grimaced and then felt a little embarrassed by how clearly my face had betrayed my feelings.

Adrian patted my back and said under his breath, "It's good to let the love in your heart show. However, the process of expanding your love can be painful as that portal of expression opens. Nevertheless, do not mourn for this soul, as he goes to a place where the opportunities to further develop his particular creative genius are far greater than they are here."

I was relieved to know about his future and thankful Mr. Krasnansky would be spared the last few months of physical agony.

As we approached Sister Diana and her companion, I forced myself to withhold a gasp. She showed all the signs of being a woman in her eighties even though a moment earlier she had appeared to be no more than twenty-nine years old.

She smiled up at Adrian and me and said, "Allow me to introduce you to a very dear old friend of mine. This is the famous tenor virtuoso, Leon Krasnansky. Leon, these are two other dear friends, Jonathan King and Adrian Goodfellow."

Mr. Krasnansky offered his hand to me and I shook it gently. When he saw Adrian, a strange look came over his face. "You remind me a great deal of a young man I once knew in my native home of Moscow before I began my singing career. If you were dressed in peasants' clothes I could swear you were he as he looked when we were both very young. At that time he was my greatest inspiration. He gave me hope which allowed me to push past a horrible stutter I had suffered from since childhood. He helped me to face my fear and was instrumental in encouraging my initial vocal studies. He said that once I had a chance to hear myself sing publicly without a stutter, I would soon conquer the deep insecurities that lay behind my disability. As you might know, he was correct.

"What a wonderful memory you have brought back to me, Mr. Goodfellow! And this in addition to meeting my dear Sister Diana who was my only friend when I was a child! None of the other children wanted to play with a funny little boy who sounded so absurd. They would tease and taunt me whenever I tried to join in. But she was my friend and she loved me just the way I was. You are a very fortunate gentlemen to have a friend like her."

As he finished his heart-rending recollection, he breathed a deep sigh of contentment, closed his eyes and relaxed into his chair.

Adrian leaned over Sister Diana and they both held his hands and smiled with the most deeply loving expression I had ever seen. I brushed a tear from my cheek and sighed deeply as a wonderfully warm feeling coursed through my body.

"Rest now, old friend, rest," Adrian said softly. "Soon you will wake to see the true greatness of what you have accomplished and the thousands of souls you have lifted with the love that poured through your beautiful music. It was the same love that helped to lift you out of your disability, the love that lives in each of us."

I looked at Adrian in awe as the realization of his true relationship to Mr. Krasnansky became apparent to me. "You were the friend and mentor he spoke of," I said in astonishment.

Sister Diana, who had resumed her previous youthful appearance, addressed my growing bewilderment. "Our brother Leon saw me as he expected to see me. When he was a child I appeared to be a mature woman, much as I looked to you as a child, so I would have to have aged. We did not want to alarm him during his final Earthly hours. We came to lessen his suffering with happy memories that would assist him in making a peaceful transition into Reality. He will sleep now and awaken on the other side where we will be waiting to guide him into a brighter world of growth and fulfillment."

Once again I sighed and shook my head. "Every moment I am with you two is like a dream, a dream too good to be true. I almost expect it to end at any minute and wake up to find that I have been snoozing at my drafting board."

"In a much more real sense than you can now imagine, you and most of humanity have been asleep at the drafting board of life. Only now, as the brilliant wave of awakening approaches, will people see that all designs a person carries with strongly focused will and passion eventually come to fruition," Adrian noted.

Instantly, the vision I had seen earlier filled my mind. The wave of light appeared again, except that it was not a vision but a reality. I seemed to be riding atop a giant wave of living light moving at incredible speed through space toward the Earth, with the sunlike disk in between. All around me were twinkling stars, and in the distance, I could see the entire solar system. Although I had the impression that great distances separated me from the solar system, I could clearly see the planets revolving around the sun. It was as if I were simultaneously in the middle of the solar system and somehow also at an immense distance away from it.

These images occupied my thoughts for only a moment, because what caught my attention was a thick and ugly dark gray cloud completely surrounding the Earth. The planet didn't look at all like the pictures shot by astronauts from space. As I looked more closely, I noticed thousands of little dots of light across the planet. Deep within my heart I felt that the wave of light I was riding was in some way connected with the dots of light. I also felt a subtle pull by the tiny lights on the giant wave of light hurtling toward Earth.

"You might wish to wear swimming trunks next time, dearheart," Sister Diana teased as the vision disappeared and I found myself back on the aircraft with my friends.

"Wow!" I felt awed by what I had seen. Then I readjusted to my surroundings and sank into an empty seat to ponder the images I had just experienced. "What does it mean? I now have an idea of what the vision symbolized based upon what I have learned recently. And it seems obvious now that the gold stone amulet you gave me when I was a child was a link to my intuition and is also related to the sunlike disk in my visions. But it's all so fantastic! I certainly would appreciate it if you two would shed some light on the subject." I was gratified that everything was out in the open and that I would finally get some answers.

Adrian sat in another empty seat across the aisle from me as Sister Diana stood leaning against the back of my seat. No one seemed to notice them. Sister Diana began to unravel the mystery that had become such a powerful influence on me.

"What you were first seeing with your inner eyes and have now actually experienced is an enormous vibration of light, or awakening, that is fast approaching your planet. The actual arrival time, by Earthly measurement, will be determined by the strength of the many dots of light you saw peeking through the dark cloud currently wrapped around Mother Earth. The dots of light increase the velocity of the wave and hasten the arrival of the new planetary awareness that is coming. The effects are already being felt as the link between the wave and the dots of light becomes stronger.

"It is a time of gathering, a period when the lightbearers of the planet, also known as wayshowers, are joining together to herald the new awakening and to pave the way for those who are blinded by the clouds of darkness and illusion now covering the Earth. It is a time of great hope when humankind will see the promise of peace on Earth and goodwill toward others become a reality.

"However, this time does not come without a price for those who show the way and especially for those who resist the inevitable changes now rapidly advancing toward them."

A shudder ran up and down my spine. If I was to be a lightbearer or a wayshower, I did not know how it was to happen. What price would I be expected to pay? Would I be able to pay it when the time came?

"All in good time, Jonathan, all in good time," Adrian assured me with a confident smile.

I sighed with quiet frustration. Then a question I had been wanting to ask came to my mind. "Something has been bothering me about what you were saying regarding Leon Krasnansky. You said, Sister Diana, that he saw you the way he would expect you to look after many years of separation, right?" She nodded. "Then why did I first see you on the beach looking exactly as you had looked to me as a child?"

Sister Diana smiled. "Your mind was focused on the guidance Adrian had just given you about the visibility of thought, and you were focusing on the colors surrounding me rather than on my physical appearance. In addition, you had already experienced a number of shocks which we allowed to occur in order to test your resilience and your readiness for what was to come. Although they were disturbing, we relied on the years of preparation that had been going on since you were a child and on your strong creative link with Spirit to pull you through those jolts. All of that has led you to the level of understanding you now have."

"So what you are saying is that I have been prepared and trained since childhood to be part of a band of wayshowers who will usher in this great wave of light, or awareness, that is approaching the Earth. Is that it?"

Both Sister Diana and Adrian smiled warmly and nodded. "This is a moment we have steadily worked toward with deep love and humility. We have dedicated ourselves to the moment when you would finally see your true destiny and join us in this vital and noble work," Sister Diana replied.

I had experienced firsthand the benefits that could be derived from contact with my wayshower friends. I trembled at the thought of what could have become of me without the friendship of dear Sister

Diana at that critical period in my life when I was an orphan. As unreachable, withdrawn and lonely as I had been, the potential for a life of lost dreams, wasted talent and possible self-destruction had been more than probable. Just as millions of other children did, I, too, could easily have drifted aimlessly into a life of mind-numbing drugs, shallow experiences and self-indulgence in an attempt to salve the wounds of a childhood barren of loving care and attention. I wondered how many children had been denied the blessing I was offered.

"Many," Adrian answered, as if I had asked the question out loud. "Many, dear Jonathan. A very wise teacher once said, 'Many are called, but few are chosen.' That is why it is so important for those who do have understanding to share it with those who are void of it. However, just as an athlete prepares for an important contest, one must prepare oneself and not leave any dark corners that could attract distortions of the light or that could even destroy the goodness that could have been."

I considered the opportunity that lay before me with more than a little trepidation, wrestling with the self-doubt that made me fear I would be unable to measure up to my friends' lofty example. A wave of anxiety passed through my midsection.

"How can I ever come close to the accomplishments you two have shown me? I am only a man, one with many faults," I moaned.

"As were we once," Sister Diana replied. "We are no different from you except in our understanding of our true inheritance and the incredible power at our fingertips. It is not just for a privileged few but for everyone who will allow the scales of illusion and limitation to fall from their eyes. Just as you must now do, we began where we were when our eyes were opened and grew from there."

"We were once just like you," Adrian added, "and others who had gone on a little farther stepped down from their lofty levels of reality and showed us the way. From then on, we had many opportunities to express the limitless creativity that lies within each of those who will cooperate with Spirit. We chose to share what we had learned with many like you, Jonathan, who showed immediate potential and could be trusted with the powerful secrets of the first and second Millennium Tablets.

"And yet, over thousands of years, those secrets have been known to many who were given the opportunity to bear the light and guide humanity through its evolution back to Spirit. The secrets were often shrouded in symbolism and taught in whatever hidden societies were appropriate to the culture and the level of evolution of people at the time. But now, as the wave of new awareness fast approaches the planet, these secrets will become available, open and simple for the great mass of humanity to comprehend.

"It is the dark, selfish forces of the planet that took the secrets and misused their power. They do not wish these simple truths to be given to the world, for then their long-standing control of the very body, mind and soul of each human will be lost."

"You said a moment ago that you chose to work with people who showed 'immediate' potential. Well, you guys have been plodding along with me since my childhood. Do you call that immediate?" I was still a little confused.

"Remember, Jonathan," Sister Diana reminded me, "time and space are of Earthly understanding and are part of the great illusion. I will try to illustrate.

"Before a person is born, he is given a blueprint, or pattern, for his life, much like the pattern a seamstress might use to create an article of clothing. The pattern represents the parameters, or boundaries, of the fate so many people feel they are chained to. However, if the pattern were perfectly completed during a person's lifetime, which was the soul's original intent, the finished garment would be far more beautiful than the person could imagine. Unfortunately, through the illusion of limitation which manifests as fear, self-doubt, insecurity, hatred, prejudice, intolerance, separation and many other dark attitudes, the pattern usually evolves in a less than flawless fashion. That creates, for the hapless seamstress, distress, disillusionment, disease of body and mind and poverty of spirit —

regardless of whether the outward circumstances are lofty or degraded.

"But we can see the end from the beginning, for to us all is the present. We look only at the perfectly completed whole and allow no thought of limitation to destroy that truth. Naturally, it takes patience and practice to acquire such an ability, but everyone can and will achieve it eventually."

"But how do you explain your ability — and I suppose mine as well — to just sort of drop into any time frame you choose?" I inquired, wanting desperately to get a firm grip on the subject.

Adrian gave me another analogy. "Let us, for example, say the pattern of life is one of your musical laser disks. And let us say that we are viewing all of the music from above. As we look down on it, we see the entirety of the lifetime. We do not see it in a linear fashion, one circumstance after another, but if we need to, we can take the laser light of our consciousness and place it at a particular point on the disk. We will find the identical phrase of music (or life circumstance) playing there if we focus on exactly the same point each time.

"However, each person has free will and can alter the music on the disk, making it more beautiful or, conversely, ugly and out of tune. That's how a wayshower can assist a person: help in making correct and positive decisions does not interfere with free will."

By then, I was beginning to have a clear understanding and I became very excited.

"So in order to drop into any time frame, as you put it, all you need to do is see life from an elevated vantage point, or consciousness, and place your thoughts on the exact spot to be dropped into. As I said, everyone has free will within the pattern, so although the end is known from the beginning, the circumstances along the way can vary greatly."

Not being able to further contain my enthusiasm as the light of understanding was upon me, I jumped into the narrative.

"So each and every individual is headed for a similar magnificent awareness but, along the way, each will encounter varying degrees of difficulty or suffering due to the illusion of limitation. The way-showers can reduce the suffering through their love and guidance. Is that it?" I grinned gleefully.

"That's it. And never has there been a time in history when their influence has been more valuable than now, during the arrival of the wave of light-awareness on the planet," Sister Diana concluded. Then on a lighter note she teased, "Now that you've heard the job description, how do you feel about joining the company?"

Although Sister Diana and Adrian were consistently dealing with serious material in their discussions, they always had a sense of humor and seemed never to take themselves too seriously.

"Well, if you have taken this much time and trouble to work with me, you must feel I have what it takes, so I guess I'll give it a try," I answered, noting a knot in my stomach and excitement in my heart.

13

ALL THINGS ARE POSSIBLE

JUST AS I FINISHED SPEAKING, THE MOVIE SCREEN LIT UP IN THE cabin section in which we were sitting. Before the movie began, Sister Diana spoke to me in a very serious tone.

"Jonathan, you must do much more than try. You must act! It is necessary to have an unshakable faith in your ability to carry through whatever projects you select in order for them to reach successful manifestation. You must approach each objective with responsibility, for many people will be relying on your steadfastness. Great harm can be done by those who have pure, unselfish motives but insufficient diligence and courage to achieve their goals. A half-hearted attempt to attain a worthy ideal can be devastating to those who believed in the guidance they had been given."

At that point images began to appear on the screen, and the first scene showed a long line of vehicles heading into an enormous parking lot. As the parade continued I had the strange sense of being drawn into the moving images. Within moments, the surrounding aircraft cabin had faded away and I found myself standing on a boulevard between parked cars and watching the lot fill up. About one hundred yards away was a gigantic domed stadium with a retract-able top that was just opening to allow the twinkling stars and balmy evening air to contribute their grandeur to the upcoming show.

The entrance to the stadium was just out of view so I began walking between the rows of parked vehicles in order to see what attraction was being presented. As I rounded the corner, I came upon my two friends dressed in ushers' uniforms. It seemed that whenever they were about to reveal to me something that was particularly shocking, they used some sort of amusing theatric and put big grins on their faces.

Adrian laughed and pointed to the electronic sign that was flickering information to the crowd. "Look, my friend, and see the work that lies before you."

My heart began pounding wildly as I read the flashing red letters that spelled out the evening's event.

LIVE TONIGHT

The First Millennium Tablet

with

Jonathan King and

There was another name beside mine but it was obscured by a flag fluttering in the wind. I assumed it probably said either Adrian or Sister Diana, so I gave it little thought at the time. There must have been sixty thousand people or more waiting to hear me and the other person speak — me, Jonathan King, architect. World-renowned Jonathan King. Dead Jonathan King. How could this be?

I looked back to where my friends had been standing but they were gone. Once again the living vision began to fade and instead of returning to my seat next to Adrian in the aircraft, I found myself in another scene.

I was in a dressing room with a woman whose back was to me. As she turned around I instantly recognized her as Cindy, Adrian's assistant during my recovery in the airport.

"Almost ready, Jonathan?"

She spoke affectionately as if she was actually talking to me. Although I was somewhat surprised, I found myself addressing her. Somehow, I was not speaking but observing myself speak. It was as if I were inside the mind of the speaker, me, and yet not actually saying the words. It was an eerie feeling, but thrilling.

"Yes, thank you, Cindy," my voice replied. "Just help me on with my suit jacket and we're ready to roll," I said with an enthusiastic laugh. The voice was definitely mine, but different. I had always had a confident way of communicating but my tone had acquired a gentle, yet commanding essence I had never possessed before, and I liked the way it felt.

"We have a full house tonight, Jonathan," she said. "The work is proceeding well, don't you think?"

"Yes, we have been blessed with another receptive audience with whom to share the emerging truth and I am very grateful for the privilege of doing my part." I noticed that although the voice was definitely powerful in its delivery there seemed to be an underlying fatigue in it.

Cindy smiled with deep affection and softly suggested, "Rest a few more minutes, Jonathan. You must save your strength."

"You are right, of course, Cindy, as always. I will close my eyes for just a few moments before we go."

As the eyes of my other self closed, I instinctively shut my own. A moment later, they blinked open and once again I found myself in the aircraft cabin watching the final credits of the in-flight movie which read

Production . . . Adrian Goodfellow
Direction . . . Sister Diana

"We thought you'd appreciate that little added touch," Sister Diana said as she and Adrian giggled.

I sat quietly for a considerable time while my friends, as usual, waited patiently for the experience to sink in. In a daze, I stared straight ahead, my vision slightly blurred. Finally, shaking my head in bewilderment, I said, "I just don't understand. How can any of this be possible? I'm supposed to be dead. That is, passed over to this side. I mean, you two showed me the plane wreck and the arm and hand sticking out of the snow with the jade ring on the finger. My hand! My ring! How can I be speaking at some giant domed stadium if I'm dead?"

Although I expressed considerable frustration in my voice, my friends remained calmly compassionate and smiled knowingly at each other. "After all you have seen and experienced with us, Jonathan, I'm a little surprised you doubt the possibility of anything," Adrian replied.

"Besides, who said you were dead?" Sister Diana added with a laugh.

I raised my head instantly at that remark and stammered incoherently. "But . . . but the crash! The frozen hand and arm! All the bodies and the wreckage! How could I have survived it?"

"You didn't. That is, you haven't yet, dearheart," answered Sister Diana. "Remember, you have free will in many matters within the boundaries of your particular life pattern. Like the accident that took the lives of your parents but not yours, there is once again a window of opportunity available to you — and, for that matter, to the world."

She paused for a moment to allow the startling news to sink in, then continued. "The time of transition out of the school of life and back to reality is foreordained as part of a soul's original life pattern. However, in certain circumstances in which an individual's growth shows promise or there has been actual attainment beyond the original pattern, a kind of extension is offered to the soul, not on a conscious level but on a higher level, such as where we are right now.

"On this level of the subconscious an individual can look down on the total record of the life he has just lived, as we have illustrated for you in part. The first window of opportunity was offered to you just before the car accident and because you chose to stay and accept the consequences that resulted, I was permitted to enter your Earth life to assist in the initial preparations for your expanded life pattern.

"Your growth has been all that we had hoped for. Your work allowed you to develop focused concentration and a strong link with your intuition. As a result, you had great success in creating the objectives you chose to focus on. In addition, your success brought to you international acclaim and a network of many powerful friends. Those associations include people of every race, color, creed and spiritual persuasion and so allow you a unique opportunity for world service at this critical turning point on Earth.

"Your purpose is to assist humankind to unite through a common objective. The peoples of the world have consistently shown an amazing ability to overcome their differences when confronted with a common obstacle. Recently, such obstacles have included uniting as allies during wartime and fighting the ravages of the ecological destruction of Mother Earth that threatens all of humanity.

"However, these unions are not restricted to fighting a common enemy; they extend to all areas of creativity. Down through the ages, people in the musical, literary, artistic and, in your case, architectural fields have forged seemingly impossible unions. Even while killing each other on the battlefield, people of two entirely opposed philosophies can embrace the same beautiful piece of music or marvel together at the magnificence of a great cathedral.

"There are, however, still greater areas yet to be explored. The rapidly approaching wave of light brings with it the inspiration to turn knowledge into spiritual understanding and awareness and thereby add wisdom to the power that knowledge has provided. Wisdom and power together will bring peace, the thousand years of peace that have been prophesied.

"In order for humankind to interpret correctly the new and powerful energies that the wave of light is bringing with it, wise, selfless, loving leadership is very much needed. It will be provided by the combined efforts of the lightbearers and wayshowers who have qualified themselves for the crucial service."

Sister Diana once again had left me awestruck. Not dead! Or maybe not dead — my decision. Influencing tens of thousands of people toward unity . . . being a wayshower . . . it was all so fantastic! How could it all be true? And yet why should I continue to doubt anything my friends told me?

During my lifetime I had been called a cross between Frank Lloyd Wright and Buckminster Fuller, for I'd been able to tear down ancient barriers and expand engineering possibilities without losing the spirit of the structure.

As layers of an onion's skin are peeled away to reveal deeper layers, the origin of creative expression became more and more clear as my friends took me more deeply into the living truth behind the appearances of life. Humans, with their finite minds, could know the infinite mind of Spirit only if they became like their Creator — infinite. The mind must therefore let go of the last vestiges of limitation and accept that all things are possible, provided Spirit is allowed to do Its work through people.

At that moment I made the commitment to pay whatever price might be asked of me. If indeed it would soon be possible for life on Earth to be as beautiful, loving and simple as life on the next level of consciousness, as demonstrated to me by Adrian and Sister Diana, then no price, no sacrifice would be too high to pay if I could be a part of helping that to happen.

As these thoughts quietly filtered into the deepest recesses of my mind, Sister Diana and Adrian carefully studied my level of commitment. The distance I had traversed between childhood and manhood had been enormous, but the growth that had occurred since my first contact with Adrian in the doomed aircraft had been almost beyond measurement — as they had hoped it would be.

However, there was still the danger that the cost of the service I was being asked to perform would shrink the courage I was experiencing. When I knew just how much I would need to give up, would I carry through? Would I be the master of the challenging task before me? These questions troubled my friends for a reason I could not suspect at the time.

Finally, I spoke. "I can't say I am without fear, my dear friends. All I can say is, lead on and I will follow, no matter what."

Sister Diana and Adrian beamed with loving pride and each of them took one of my hands. "We are confident you will face what lies ahead with all the strength you possess," Adrian said. "And be certain in your heart, dear friend, that from this moment on, we will be with you every step of the way."

14

DARK CORNERS

"THE TIME HAS COME TO SHOW YOU THE DARK SIDE OF THE POWER to create," Sister Diana began. "The confusion, conflict, distrust and even hatred that people hold with reference to religious doctrine and philosophy are motivated, in large measure, by the inequities in the world. The teachings of the various churches, temples and synagogues and other philosophies are consistent in many areas, and most share one basic tenet: Treat your fellow humans as you would like to be treated.

"All too frequently we see those with devout spirits and courageous hearts turn away when they see disproportionate abundance poured onto those who think only of themselves. The question often raised is, How can a divine being of love, no matter what he or she might be called, allow such things to happen?"

My interest sharpened as Sister Diana approached a subject that had plagued me all my life, one that had kept me out of the mainstream of organized religion, for none of the more visible teachings could give me a satisfactory answer to explain the incredible unfairness humankind had endured throughout history.

Indeed, I had tried to embrace many beliefs. Initially, it had been an easy and pleasant task, due to the extensive traveling I had done with my aunt and uncle while I was growing up. I'd had significant exposure to the various cultures of the world, which had helped me to appreciate art and architecture but more importantly had exposed me, to one degree or another, to the teachings of Judaism, Christianity, Taoism, Hinduism, Islam and a few more obscure beliefs. I'd also examined the teachings of the giants of the ages, from Aristotle and Plato to Freud and Jung. Many of the philosophies bore similarities to each other; all were worthy of respect. However, on observing the living results of those philosophies in the form of their adherents, I'd been disappointed. The followers always seemed to dilute the essence of the original teachings and they failed to live up to the high standards set by the authors. What was the point, I thought, if the teachings did not provide a safe and achievable path away from weaknesses and human frailty? Why try at all if guilt and self-degradation were the price of failure?

And yet, I had argued in my mind, civilization must have a set of rules to live by. It must have guidelines and moral codes of conduct or else it would soon sink into widespread anarchy and return to cave dwellings.

The best that could be expected, I had finally decided, was a struggle for balance and survival amid discouraging evidence of the all too common pursuit of selfish interests.

Granted, there were significant exceptions to that rule, and a few bright lights would shine from time to time in medicine or human rights or world ecology, but they appeared insignificant when stacked up against the mass of ignorance, fear and hatred that permeated every corner of the world.

So I elected to do my best to invest whatever talent and goodness there might be in myself in the concentrated pursuit of the creative expression I knew best. I felt that was not burying my head in the sand, as some might think, but, rather, it was keeping my own backyard clean and doing the best I could each day.

Certainly my contributions had been more than significant. But deep within me there had always been a void, something seriously missing from my life. There was a constant yearning to express something more that just wouldn't or couldn't come out or even make itself known to me. The frustration had grown even more poignant in recent years, so using the pretense of looking at an exclusive residential community being planned in Honolulu I took a side trip to Kauai, hoping to find a placid environment where I could take a rest and do some deep thinking.

"Have you heard about lighting one candle in the darkness?" Sister Diana asked, interrupting my reverie.

As usual, she had penetrated to the heart of my thoughts.

"Is that like saying each vote counts in an election?" I replied in a skeptical tone.

She ignored the edge in my voice, understanding the futility so many people feel when fighting a giant with a slingshot. Nevertheless, she also knew that through focused concentration on the objective, the giant could be vanquished; it was all a matter of faith.

I immediately regretted my manner and apologized humbly.

"We understand, my friend," Adrian said. "The wounds of the past rise quickly to the surface as a person makes a commitment to achieve total self-awareness. It is a dangerously critical time when a soul sees the possibility of significant self-development, yet seems repeatedly dragged down by the darkness of old habit patterns that float to the surface of consciousness. The tendency toward self-degradation or, worse, self-pity and despondency is often irresistible and can cause loss of courage at a critical moment. If the seeker could see at those times the grand opportunity for growth only a short distance away from his grasp, he would take courage, quickly learn to forgive himself and press on."

I considered the wisdom of these remarks and recalled many colleagues who had failed to reach their full potential due to excessive self-criticism and the accepting of other people's viewpoints, which had resulted in their losing their spirit for the work.

History was littered with broken dreams and failed destinies, so those who had held on to their dreams and achieved their destinies stood out like towering beacons of hope that symbolized possibility. To them, all failures were stepping stones to success. People like Albert Einstein, Thomas Edison, Nikola Tesla, Alexander Graham

Bell, Helen Keller, Mother Teresa and Mahatma Gandhi, together with thousands of unsung heroes of the human spirit, stood out as dramatic testimonies to the power of undying faith and the courage to pursue a dream.

I referred back to Sister Diana's original topic and paraphrased her solemn statement. "Your question has echoed in the hearts and souls of more people than any other since the advent of humanity on this planet: How can Spirit allow the great suffering and cruelty that exists on Earth?"

"Free will, dearheart, the great gift of free will," Sister Diana replied. "As we have already illustrated, a person has considerable latitude within the boundaries of the life pattern he calls fate. Within that latitude he makes many mistakes until finally, exhausted by the whiplash of his selfish pursuits and thoughtless cruelty, he opens up to the still, small voice of love within, the great Spirit, which then guides him into harmony, balance and peace.

"There have been periods throughout history during which an influence of greater or lesser degree has been brought to bear on humanity that has urged him toward his inevitable awakening. As we have explained and as you have seen in your living visions, an influence in the form of a light wave of enormous proportions has almost reached the Earth. With that great inspiration, the inheritance of darkness on Earth and in the hearts of men and women will soon give way to a new age of peace on Earth and of goodwill to all of humanity."

My friends allowed all the implications of free will to sink into my mind. It was true, then, that humans have always been totally responsible for their own circumstances and Spirit has held back Its power to change those circumstances people have asked for help. When assistance was asked for and help did not seem to be forthcoming, it was due to the overwhelming strength of the thought forces of those who had created the negative circumstances to begin with. And those forces had often been put into place centuries earlier and fueled by belief systems, superstitions and the illusion of being limited.

Nevertheless, no request for help or prayer had ever gone unanswered. The energy of the thought was not lost but went on to the scales of cause and effect, to manifest at some period, sooner or later. Patience or the lack of it had been the reason so many had lost faith in the power of prayer.

I voiced my hypothesis to my friends in a brief summary. "I believe I see a deeper meaning to the power of thought. It's a great privilege and it's an incredible responsibility. I believe I now see that Spirit has not allowed anything cruel to happen. Through the gift of free will, people have not only allowed it to happen, they have actually created it themselves."

"Excellent, my friend, excellent," Adrian congratulated me. "You have grasped the very foundation of what we have been showing you. Now we will demonstrate what happens to thoughts whose time has not yet come."

Adrian led the way up the aisle of the aircraft and Sister Diana and I followed. We stopped beside an aging man whose well-dressed appearance could not hide a soul who had forsaken all hope, who had cast his destiny to the wind and seen it blown away by the whirlwind of a cruel circumstance, a fate of which he himself had been the architect.

By then it had become apparent to me that the passengers could not see us, and I wondered how Leon Krasnansky had been able to do so.

"Your own histories of dying — or, as we prefer to call it, transition — are filled with people who have claimed to hear, see and even interrelate with visitors unseen to others present at the time. Those testimonies usually occurred close to the time of transition." I nodded in agreement as Adrian continued.

"They are fellow wayshowers who are permitted to descend to the Earth plane briefly to help to make the final hours or minutes of passing gentle, welcome and peaceful. Thousands of lovers, relatives and acquaintances have testified that they have witnessed miraculous changes in the attitude of the departing person. They have often noticed an illumination around the face of a person just before his transition.

"When such visitations do occur, they are often prompted by a soul's readiness to leave. But more frequently the channel is already there, usually having been constructed out of a life of service and love. You would be surprised, Jonathan, how many people are prepared months in advance in this way, and many meet their transition through means other than sickness."

I considered this fascinating information for a moment, then asked, "What about older people whose minds have left them or those in comas with no hope of regaining consciousness?"

Sister Diana had a deeply compassionate expression on her face as if she'd had considerable first-hand experience with such cases. "Many have indeed suffered over a loved one who, it seemed, would be better off passing on quickly. Yet often they hang on for years, causing deep distress and hardship to the attending relatives and friends. But there is a beautiful silver lining behind such situations.

"Deep contemplation and faith are necessary in order to comprehend them. The school of life holds an infinite number of possibilities and opportunities for spiritual growth, and Spirit never gives a soul a task it is not up to, even though it might appear otherwise.

"Therefore, the apparently tragic existence of a person who is only a shell of his previous self provides fertile ground for the development in those around him of selflessness, patience, self-sacrifice, tolerance and love. Once such qualities are truly learned, they never leave the soul who has earned them.

"Although it can be much more difficult and even dangerous, sometimes the best and quickest way up the mountain is straight up the side. And that might be exactly what the soul had helped to design into his own future life pattern to begin with. The person who is in a coma, for example, is usually in a totally different realm of consciousness and completely unaware of the deterioration of his or her body. The suffering attributed to these souls is frequently nonexistent. There are, of course, those who suffer greatly, but again, there is a purpose and an opportunity. For that soul it is easier to tune in to the great healing love of Spirit once the distractions of the material world are less easily available."

As I became enlightened by these revelations a deep urge to reach out to those who suffered needlessly overwhelmed me. Sister Diana and Adrian beamed as they observed a rosy glow swirling around my heart area.

"Now, let us return to the subject at hand, dearheart," Sister Diana urged. "I want you to focus for a moment on our discouraged friend here."

I did as I was told and observed the sagging posture of a man whose body language was expressing great self-pity, but there was no trace of bitterness that I could see, for he seemed to have burned out that useless waste of energy. He was like an empty vessel humbly waiting for the waters of life to reanimate him. Unfortunately, the dark sadness within him had sealed off his ability to receive that vital refreshment.

"Now close your eyes and continue your concentration," she said. I did so and found myself sitting on a folding wooden chair and listening, along with several hundred other people, to a dynamic speaker dressed entirely in white clothes down to his socks and shoes. We were in a giant tent apparently pitched in an open field, for under my feet was trampled grass. The speaker bellowed an emotional sermon, frequently punctuated by shouts from the audience who called out, "Praise the Lord! Hallelujah! Amen, Amen, Amen!"

The mood was electric and I noticed that the speaker controlled the crowd's responses like a master puppeteer. The slightest increase in the pitch of his voice, a gesture of his hand or even a deep sigh would send the gathered assembly into ecstatic hallelujahs.

I was fascinated by the colors I was seeing around the man. Although I had not yet learned their meanings, I was able to interpret them to some extent. The total effect registered in one instant, quite unlike the progressive thought patterns of normal observation and reason. My impression was of a man sincerely devout in his mission and well equipped, both mentally and spiritually, for his chosen task.

But what struck me most strongly was a dark hole in the colors around the preacher's midsection that interpreted itself to me as suppressed lust, lust for material and carnal things he had denied himself during his determined journey toward spiritual leadership. I felt an ominous specter of impending disaster awaiting the man, a man whose dream was rapidly unfolding, yet trailing behind that dream were the garbage bags of unresolved desire.

"If a person doesn't face his deepest temptations and subsequently release those desires, they will continually be drawn into his path. The desires, no matter how debased they may be, must be properly challenged and eliminated," said a familiar voice in the seat behind me. I turned to find Sister Diana grinning as usual, enjoying my habitual surprise at finding my friends dropping in and out of my experiences.

"Although the mind might be oblivious to an unsatisfied need or desire lurking beneath its conscious awareness, the object of that desire is being magnetically attracted to the individual just as powerfully as it would be if he were aware of it, and he will be exposed time and again to temptations that offer to fulfill the hidden desire until it is submitted to or else faced and conquered once and for all time.

"That is why it is impossible for a soul who is not fully awakened to judge another individual with any degree of accuracy. A person looking through his own dark glass does not know what remains hidden within himself. Additionally, he is often incapable of seeing the great goodness lying beneath the surface of those people he is so quick to condemn."

I nodded my head. Sister Diana stood up and moved into the aisle and toward the exit of the tent. I followed her to the canvas flap that served as a door and, pushing it aside, we walked through the opening. But instead of finding the field on which the tent had been raised, we were in a television studio.

"Now understand, dearheart, that I am not in any way endorsing the indulgence of every debased fantasy a soul might have. What I am saying is that the desires must be faced and overcome, and that can be accomplished by learning from other people's experience or by going through it oneself. The former is infinitely less painful and much quicker."

We moved through the studio, apparently unseen by the technicians on the floor or by the studio audience as they filed in and took their seats. A woman dressed in a purple choir robe began to sing a hymn, accompanied by an unseen organist. The lights dimmed almost to and then a spotlight beamed on a curtain on the opposite side of the set.

As the hymn reached an emotional crescendo, a white-clad man holding a white Bible strode onto the stage. The crowd wailed, "Hallelujah," and the preacher displayed a perfect set of capped teeth in response to the adulation. "Praise the Lord, dear brethren, we have moved over the top!" A drum roll accompanied him as he shouted at the top of his voice and pointed to a twelve-foot thermometer with dollar amounts indicated on it. The green core was completely filled, and at the top, flashing red lights announced that twenty million dollars had been raised. The audience screamed its approval, chanting, "Hallelujah, Praise the Lord."

The scene faded and a few seconds later, Sister Diana, Adrian and I were standing in the Sun beside an enormous swimming pool. The preacher was lying on a patio lounge chair and speaking into a cellular phone.

"Yes, that's right, Goldstein. I said buy fifty thousand shares for my private account. I don't know what they would think if they knew, but they're not going to know, are they Goldstein? Stop worrying and let me get off this phone, will ya? I've got company waiting for me. What? No, not Kathy," he said under his breath. "It's Angela!" He laughed. "Remember? Yeah, that's the one." He waved at Angela, still laughing, and cut off the line.

"Aren't you ready yet, honey?" Angela pouted in her teenage voice.

"You bet I am, Sweet Pea. Here comes daddy!" The preacher

jumped out of his lounge chair and swinging his hips and giggling, jogged the few yards over to the adolescent. He wrapped his arms around her, pulled her close and gave her a long, deep kiss. Then they turned and walked hand in hand toward the sliding glass doors that led to the bedroom.

Once again the scene changed and we were sitting on the back benches of a courtroom. A man in a white suit was standing in front of a sullen-faced judge.

"You have displayed heinous behavior in betraying the innocent trust of the millions who have had faith in your leadership. The funds you expropriated for your own selfish ends were given to you for a much higher purpose, a purpose you have degraded by displaying the self-same conduct it was your mission to overcome.

"Have you anything to say for yourself before I pass judgment on you?"

The man in the white suit bowed his head in shame and slowly nodded his head indicating he wished to speak. He turned to face the crowded courtroom and the cameras that were silently delivering their fallen idol to the millions who had supported his meteoric rise to fame.

"Brothers and sisters — if I may still be permitted to address you as such, for in my heart you remain so to me — I have sinned a great sin. I, who have led you into the glory beyond, have fallen from your grace, for I, too, am only a man." His voice choked back tears as he continued. "We cannot serve two masters and yet we must face both before we choose one or the other. Years ago, when I chose my path of endeavor, I failed to do that and I left some dark doors unopened, doors that now have swung wide, allowing your humble servant to be claimed by the devil. Pray for me, dear brethren, for indeed, Hell is where I am!"

The courtroom was filled with the sniffles and sobs of the still-faithful followers who continued to offer their support. That time, however, only amens were heard.

Then I was back on the airplane standing with Sister Diana and

Adrian beside the lonely and saddened figure of a man who had once led millions in spiritual growth.

"And what do you say of our friend, here, Jonathan, now that you have seen this brief review of his rise and fall?"

I contemplated what I had witnessed, then looked down at the figure slumped in his airline seat. "I feel much different from the way I would have felt before I met you two. I am certain I would have condemned this sort of fellow out of hand with the same severity the judge was exercising. However, now I perceive a higher purpose to the events leading to his downfall.

"For the followers themselves there was nothing essentially wrong in listening to a man who taught them to have faith, to forgive their enemies and to love one another. Such teachings, whatever form they take, lead to a common positive goal — the brotherhood of man. If nothing else, the followers have learned to pursue the teachings and not the teacher, to focus on the ideal and not the idol.

"But for our fallen idol, I feel that with a little forgiveness by others and by him of himself, soon his scars will heal and he will be ready to move on to even greater attainment, cleansed of the handicaps that brought him to his knees."

As I finished speaking, I thought to myself, Where did that come from? Sister Diana swiftly provided the answer.

"It came from the higher part of yourself that is now surfacing within your consciousness. As you release your personality more and more to the light of its wisdom you will experience a clarity you never before imagined possible. It is the Spirit that lives within all of us. It is the drop of water that eventually returns to the ocean of wisdom, love and power. It is the reality behind the salvation of humanity."

My heart was filled with a glowing sensation I had never experienced before. It was a feeling of profound release, as if I had just shed a skin that had fulfilled its purpose. Beneath that useless, discarded covering glowed the pink membrane of new life, perfect and fresh, yet vulnerable in its infancy.

Adrian and Sister Diana understood what was occurring and also realized that the time of birth was a dangerous one in which the newborn baby must be carefully nourished and protected until it had found itself and gathered its own strength. I felt the emanations of loving protection my friends were sharing with me. It was the same peaceful security a child feels in the caring arms of loving parents.

15

THE LOVE OF A CHILD

WHILE WE WALKED TOWARD THE FIRST-CLASS CABIN I REFLECTED on the fate of the man in white. Soon he would join the host of unseen inhabitants of a higher plane of expression. He would see the good works he had begun with a clearer perspective because of his detached viewpoint. He would review the temptations as they approached, engaged him and brought about his downfall.

Even the most barbaric events in the school of life, when viewed from a higher awareness, healed and left behind only the lessons of truth. In the gentle, peaceful environment of timelessness and love, healing was always as immediate as self-forgiveness. Once that healing occurred, the truth left behind would remain with a soul forever. There was indeed a kindly purpose to darkness. The resistance of a person against his obstacles brought about his eventual growth into light. Nothing was wasted in the cycling mosaic of Spirit's universe.

In fact, the only real sadness was the unnecessary suffering endured by humans as they reaped the fruits of their own choices, choices made in resistance to their own intuitive guidance that always suggested the quickest, easiest road to peace and love.

"All may choose," Sister Diana offered as a conclusion to my introspection. "All may choose the high road or the low road. And yet all roads lead to truth, no matter what the distance or the trials endured. All finally unite in the infinite cosmic ocean of love where all is one."

"And the privilege of shortening that distance, reducing the load and lifting part of the suffering from the shoulders of humankind is the wonderful blessing bestowed upon the worthy wayshower," Adrian added.

Before I could comment on these wonderfully uplifting words of hope, Sister Diana stopped beside a young girl of about ten years of age. She had blond hair pulled into a cute ponytail by a flowery plastic barrette, her eyes were bright blue and she wore a pretty yellow, red and orange flowered dress with matching sandals. She was holding two intricately carved tiny jade statues. One of them depicted an ancient sagelike character standing with outstretched arms. The other was a younger man on bended knee with his head bowed as if in prayer. She smiled endearingly as she gently handled the gifts she had received from a friend while visiting Asia.

Something about her was magnetic despite her tender years and I was profoundly drawn to her. Then a bolt of sadness shot through me as I remembered the fate that soon would befall the sweet child, and I wondered at the reason for such a seemingly wasteful loss.

"You are thinking with your worldly senses, dearheart," Sister Diana said. "Look beyond the youthful body at the powerful spirit you sensed beneath it, and see from a higher awareness. Within this young body dwells a very old soul. You felt that special quality as you first approached her."

I sat down in the empty aisle seat next to the child and waited for Sister Diana to continue. I was deeply interested in what she would say since I, like so many others, had always been confused and angry about the loss of innocent children through senseless acts of violence, through accident or sickness. My feelings were strong and I realized the impossibility of clear perception when my mind was clouded by the murky waters of emotional judgment, but I had always felt I couldn't help that. I wished I could but that was the way it was.

"You must will it, Jonathan. As we have told you, wishing is a useless investment of energy. For the time being, however, let us review the brief Earth history of this dear sweet soul.

"Her name is Noël and she was born into a poor family. Despite the poverty of the household, warm hearts beat within it. For years her parents were childless and had given up all hope of having a family until they received the joyous news that our little friend would be born.

"During her years on Earth, Noël has enjoyed few worldly comforts, but an enduring wealth of love preserved the family. The love that existed in the family before her arrival doubled when she came into her parents' lives and has grown ever since. Each person Noël has met has been touched by the charm that emanated from her pure heart, a heart that has accepted all as equal. Noël's love of living things has filled her days. Notwithstanding their love for her, her parents were simple people with the normal tendencies toward prejudice, but the child saw only good and spoke with the simple wisdom of sages in defending the light she saw in everyone.

"One day Noël heard a news commentator say that there was great evil in the people who live on the other side of the world and that they wanted to hurt her country's people. But she did not believe the story. Without the knowledge of her family or teachers, Noël wrote a letter to 'the leader of the people on the other side of the world.' She wrote of the love she had for everyone and how she was sure that all people would feel the same if they could just not be afraid to say that to each other. She told the leader about the news story and how she didn't believe it and said that he should tell the people in her country the real story so they wouldn't think he was bad. Noël finished by saying she knew her people were good people, too, and that they would listen. She wanted to be sure he would be encouraged by her letter because she didn't want him to be sad. She signed the letter with all her love and put several Xs and Os at the bottom.

"On the front of the envelope Noël printed her full name and address and sent the letter to 'The leader of our friends on the other side of the world.'"

I was touched by Sister Diana's story and assumed it was finished, for there could be no way a letter would arrive addressed in that way. But I did wonder what Noël was doing on the aircraft by herself, returning from somewhere east of the United States.

"All things are possible through faith," Adrian's words penetrated my skeptical thoughts. "This child's simple faith and love opened the doors for us to help. The letter arrived at its intended destination.

"Not long afterwards, her parents received a strange phone call. At first they thought it was a practical joke played by one of their friends, but soon the caller convinced them he was indeed the President of the United States, and he wanted to speak with their daughter Noël.

"Soon she was winging her way to the other side of the world on a mission of peace, invited by its leader. The world will eventually learn of that historic meeting and of the great wisdom of a child who loved everyone. News of the crash of the plane on which she had been a passenger will draw the two countries together even more closely than would have otherwise been the case. The child's involvement in the crash will create significant additional publicity and serve as common ground, becoming a powerful springboard for the development of peaceful negotiations between the two countries. It will also open even more significant doors which, at this point, you cannot even suspect.

"Love, when combined with a profound and unselfish concern or sadness, has a deep and binding permanency about it that can bridge any gap and heal any wound."

I listened in awe. Then a thought struck me.

"Yes, Jonathan, little Noël is a wayshower."

As Sister Diana said that, the child turned her head and looked straight into my eyes. I could have sworn I was looking at the face of an aging woman. The illusion, if indeed it was an illusion, gave me the impression of two faces overlapping one another, one face that of a child of ten and the other that of an ancient lady.

"The power of love has many faces, Jonathan," the adult-child said. "It fills the requirements of the need at the time. You need to see a physically mature face to justify the unusual events in the story you have just been told."

"You can see me!" I exclaimed.

"I have seen you since you were born, my brother, as I have seen many other wayshowers at various stages of their awakening."

Her form had completely changed to that of an elderly woman. She had a strong, proud face of commanding beauty with white-blond hair that flowed to her shoulders. Her blue eyes had the same mysterious glow that Adrian's and Sister Diana's eyes had but they also possessed the childlike quality I had seen a moment earlier. I felt awed by what I had just witnessed and a deeply humble respect for the truth I had been allowed to share.

"I am certain you will agree, Jonathan, that it is a very great loss when the simple faith children have in the inherent good in life leaves them when they begin to grow up. The world would have them believe it is necessary for survival to think with fearful suspicion of their fellow human beings."

As she said these words, an exciting thought occurred to me. Adrian and Sister Diana were watching me with patient knowing as a new light broke in my consciousness. "A wayshower can be anyone! It could be a king, a laborer, a policeman, a secretary or even a small child. Anyone! A person's position in life is important only to the extent that it serves the purpose of the service to be given. Therefore, many humble, seemingly insignificant lives might in fact be of enormous value when seen as part of the greater purpose, as a piece of a giant puzzle. And all the pieces of the puzzle are of importance to the integrity and completion of the whole."

The three of them were beaming so proudly that I felt my heart overflow with love and newfound awareness. I stood up and the four of us sort of huddled together in an embrace that seemed to last forever. When we separated, I brushed tears from my eyes and quietly sat down again.

Mother Noël took my right hand and turned it over, palm up. She placed in it the small jade statue of the kneeling man given to her by the leader of the other side of the world and said in a solemn voice, "Dear friend, if I may call you such" — I gave her a wide smile and nodded my head — "please take this amulet, which is symbolic of peace and loving service, and keep it with you always." She took my fingers and closed them around the amulet, making my hand into a fist. Then she leaned forward and kissed me on the forehead no less tenderly than a loving mother would kiss her baby. Although it hadn't been stated, I sensed I had just reached a major plateau and the brief gift-giving ceremony had crowned the graduation.

I thanked her softly and joined Sister Diana and Adrian as they walked back down the aisle toward the rear of the plane. When I looked over my shoulder for a last glance, I saw a sweet little blond, pony-tailed girl chatting up a storm with a cabin attendant. Then I looked down to inspect the gift Mother Noel had just given me. When I opened my hand, I gasped. The jade amulet had been replaced by a small gold stone engraved with the figures MT-II.

16

FACING FEAR

"WOW! MY MIND IS EXPLODING WITH ALL THE NEW CONCEPTS I'M being exposed to."

"We are never given anything we cannot handle," Adrian replied, "although we may elect through our free will to avoid the opportunity to learn. These opportunities come in the form of service to others, challenges to be faced or, in your case, through direct absorption of the lessons learned by others. That is the fastest way of growing and it must be accompanied by a mind that has been expanded and that retains the capacity to be disciplined.

"A person can run but he cannot hide. The lessons to be learned will return again and again. Sometimes they will wear a different mask to disguise themselves. They might come as a delightful distraction. They might wear the clothes of a severe crisis or they could cloak themselves as an exciting challenge. Other times the needed growth will come again and again in the same form until finally, and after much frustration, it is recognized for what it is and faced and overcome.

"The degree of awareness dictates the form the lesson will take, but the lessons must be faced until the final battle has been won and the last limitation conquered. That is when each person rises above his little self and takes his rightful place as a cocreator with Spirit."

I listened quietly with the deep respect I had developed for the kindly soul. As usual, Adrian's words struck at the heart of the matter, always gentle but direct, allowing for nothing but perfect understanding.

Sister Diana waved us toward the back of the plane where a cabin attendant was maneuvering the occupant of a wheelchair back into his seat. She did it in a few swift movements, and as she turned around, I saw that it was Cindy, the nurse who had helped Adrian attend to the bump on my head and who had appeared in one of my visions.

Funny, I thought. By our current timetable, that hasn't even happened yet.

The amusing thought quickly left my mind as the three of us stopped beside the disabled man. A shudder passed through my body when I saw the full extent of the man's deformity. The pants he wore could not hide the spindly sticks that served as legs, long since useless for anything but cosmetic appearance. His left arm was bent up tightly, closing the space between his upper arm and his forearm. The hand, withered and pasty, hung loosely from his wrist. His head was bent forward at a slight angle and twisted to the right so I could see his eyes. His right arm seemed to be the only part of him that was whole and complete.

I was feeling an uncontrollable urge to vomit. Ever since I could remember, something deep inside of me had abhorred anything that lacked symmetry and balance. My architectural work had been based on a creative motivation to express harmony and beauty in a functional format. However, an even deeper reason for my passion, at the time unknown to me, was lying buried within my consciousness, a memory too gruesome for my mind to accept.

A gentle hand grasped mine and my physical discomfort vanished immediately. Guilt quickly replaced it as I felt shame for the feelings that had prompted the nausea.

"Your shame is noble but misplaced, Jonathan, for the root of your discomfort has been hidden from your conscious awareness for most of your life." Sister Diana instructed me to sit in an empty seat beside the disabled man, who appeared to have fallen asleep. I did so but with considerable hesitation, for a sensation of terror was quickly swelling within me.

"By now you are clearly aware that the spirit that animates this body is inherently no different from yours or mine. The choice of the vehicle was his before his birth and it has served his life pattern well, for it helped to drive his mind deeply inward. You will note a parallel in your own life. The method used to accomplish this invaluable development of the mind was unfortunate in your case and horrendous in this soul's case — that is, from a limited human perspective. But when viewed from the greater vantage point, the sacrifice occurred in the twinkling of an eye and the benefit derived remains forever.

"You are now ready, dear friend, to face the cause of the prejudice you feel toward an aspect of the ugliness in the world. In order to lead you must first see Spirit in everything. As we have told you, love is the cohesive force that binds the universe together, and nothing can exist without its presence. The fact that most people do not yet see Spirit in their brothers and sisters, much less in themselves and every other thing on Earth does not diminish its existence."

Sister Diana put her right hand over my eyes and told me to relax and breathe deeply. She placed her left hand on my solar plexus. Soon I felt I was drifting, conscious yet euphoric, in a sea of translucent green light. It was a wonderful sensation. All cares, all anxieties, all wounds seemed to melt away. It was not that they were gone but that their potency as a source of discomfort had disappeared.

My sense of awareness seemed to grow sharper as the legion of forgotten little worries in the back of my mind fell away. "What have I been so uptight about?" I wondered.

Many petty concerns began rising to the top of my consciousness and passing before my inner eye. Intuitively, I knew that these hidden items, all some years old and completely buried in my mind, were leaving me as they paraded by: an unpaid loan of fifty dollars I'd forgotten to repay a good friend; an insult made by a critic twenty years before in panning a building I had designed; a hit-and-run driver who had scraped my first brand-new car just as I left the showroom; an argument with a contractor that had never been resolved; and the biggest guilt, one I had carried for years, a broken engagement to the only woman I had ever loved, a woman who had disliked what she saw as my excessive absorption in my work. On and on the images came, some significant and deeply painful, others incredibly petty and bordering on the ridiculous. It was like a movie review of my life's unfinished business.

But as the images passed by, I felt a healing, a sense of inner forgiveness of the issues, of the people involved and of myself, forgiveness that washed into every corner of my soul. I felt lighter and lighter, enormously relieved of a weight I had not even realized had been dragging me down.

Finally, I found myself watching a scene that startled me and immediately snapped me to attention. First I saw a deep valley below. Then I realized I was looking out of the open window of a car as it moved down a mountain road. I turned and saw my parents as they had looked when I was a child. They were laughing and chatting about holiday plans they had made.

As with some of the other visions I had experienced, the image became three-dimensional. I realized I was actually in the car watching the small boy I used to be. And the scene I dreaded and had buried deep within my mind was about to be relived, the incident that would dramatically turn the tide of my life.

"No! No, I can't go through this! Please take me back! I can't stand it! Take me back," I pleaded.

"You must face this long-buried wound and heal the scar it left behind, Jonathan. There can be no further growth until you have relived the trauma and let it go." In my mind, I heard Adrian gently encouraging me.

I took a deep breath as the car rounded a sharp curve, skidded sideways and flipped over. I was thrown through the open window into a clump of bushes. As the dust and the flying rocks and the branches of small trees settled, I noticed there was no movement at all in the car. Somehow, I was drawn to move closer to the tangled wreck and as I did so I felt a familiar presence just behind me. I turned and there beside me was the small boy I had been. At first I was surprised and confused. Then I remembered my out-of-body experience of floating above the trees when I had first seen the peregrine falcon. I must have been jolted out of my body when I was thrown from the car and then, with the normal curiosity of a child, gone to see what had happened.

The boy moved closer to the wreck but just beyond the mangled car he stopped short. I could no longer see him but instead was seeing what he was seeing. There inside the tangle of metal that moments before had been an automobile were the broken and bloodied bodies of my mother and father. I felt the small boy whose body I was now sharing let out a piercing scream.

The scene ended abruptly and I was back drifting in the pastel-green sea of light. Gently and slowly, the cutting edge of the pain I had just relived began to fade. The healing had begun to work its calming magic and I let the horror leave me forever.

I wasn't sure how long I remained in that euphoric state but it felt like hours. I experienced a wonderful release that resulted in a living sense of perfect peace that all was well within myself, all was well with the world, all was well with the universe. All was in perfect, synchronous harmony.

If only all of humanity could feel what I feel right now, so much suffering would end instantly, I thought.

"A consciousness must be ready to receive, my friend." Adrian's voice echoed in some distant recess of my mind. "The garden of the soul must be focused on love and be open to the many tools used by Spirit to lead it to love before the seeds of peace will grow.

"The truth could stand out like the Rock of Gibraltar right in front of a person possessing insufficient receptivity and he would miss it completely, as history has proven many times. Every minute of every day the greater portion of humankind reacts in exactly that manner to the living truth of life. All around there is beauty, courage, compassion, forgiveness, love and the magical cycle of unending life. From the microcosmic conscious life of the cellular structure within the human body to the macrocosmic infinity of the universe, the cycle of life continues, guided by a most benevolent, loving consciousness.

"That consciousness surpasses description, but it can be recognized by everyone once the proper state of awareness exists. Preparation for that state of awareness has, until now, been born primarily out of great suffering; in turn, that suffering has been created out of a misguided use by the human being of his free will.

"What good is a state of perfection if it is simply handed to an unconscious entity? Free will is a gift and it is also the source of the price that must be paid. Eventually, the human attains a conscious awareness of the perfection he has always possessed.

"Limitation is an illusion contrived by humanity. It falls away, as dead leaves drop from a tree, in due season. There have always have been and there always will be those who go a little farther, those who know that all growth is solely dependent on the degree to which they serve those who possess less awareness. They are like funnels that receive the light of truth and readily pour their contents upon all who are willing to receive. And in that act of emptying themselves they become free to receive even greater enlightenment. The pouring out of light and life attracts light and life. The giving of love attracts love. Likewise, those who knowingly or unknowingly use this power for selfish ends attract in exact proportion a harvest of hate and lust and greed.

"Therefore, dear friend, for those of us who have awareness, whether we have possessed it for eons or have just recently achieved it, it is a great privilege to reach down wherever and whenever we can to help short-circuit the needless round of suffering, thereby helping humanity to achieve enlightenment more quickly and easily."

Adrian's voice drifted farther and farther away as his loving words helped my understanding to expand. In the peaceful bliss I was experiencing I felt I could accept anything that was asked of me, without fear, anxiety or reservation. As that thought slipped like delicate silk through my mind, a familiar scene began to crystallize before my inner vision.

I saw the macabre mountainside setting, the tangled aircraft wreckage, the human carnage strewn across the snow, and again I saw the bizarre statuelike arm and hand protruding from the snow, clutching a blue flight bag. As I watched the vivid scene of horror unfold, I saw two of the rescuers trudge through the snow toward the frozen arm. When they reached it, they crouched down and began digging into the ice-encrusted surface with short shovels. After a few layers of hard white crust were removed, both men hit something solid. Brushing away some softer snow, they revealed an inverted aircraft seat.

The two men were then joined by two other rescuers who must have seen the discovery and recognized the possibility that survivors were buried under the wreckage. Within fifteen minutes the snow was completely removed and the team began prying apart several icebound seats. Half an hour later, they found a man lying on his side and covered with blue airline blankets. His arm was frozen solid, wedged firmly between two seats, and the airline bag was still tightly clutched in his fist. One of the workers noticed that the arm was broken close to the shoulder.

"The poor guy's arm must have been broken when he tried to pull the seats on top of himself for shelter, and before he could free it, the cold or the pain probably made him pass out."

The rescuers silently continued their grisly task and soon the body was hoisted out of its makeshift shelter and lifted onto a waiting stretcher. Suddenly, one of the men let out a loud yelp. "There's a live one here. She's alive!"

Beneath the stiff body just removed, a hole had been dug in the snow and filled with blankets. In the hole was a child almost as blue as the blankets that had served to protect her. She moaned as her eyes slowly opened a slit. A faint smile creased the corners of her mouth and she murmured something. The rescuers couldn't make it out so one of them put his ear down close to her. He listened for a minute then raised his head with a look of surprise on his face.

"Well, what did she say? What did she say?" two of the men impatiently asked at once.

He paused for a moment, then answered, "She said not to leave her friend with the others because he's still alive. Then she said we must hurry if we are to keep him alive." He shook his head in bewilderment. "I don't know how she could know, but somehow I think she's right. One of you boys go check out the guy we just hauled outta here, will ya?"

The rescuers farthest from the hole crunched off in the direction of the makeshift morgue that had been created. The remaining men returned their attention to the little girl and began checking her body for broken bones. She slowly started to come around as the warmth was gently rubbed back into her limbs by the workers.

One of the helpers asked her what her name was and how she was feeling. She said that her name was Noël and that she felt pretty good except she was cold and her head hurt. Two of the men tenderly lifted her out of her blanket-lined shelter and carried her over to a protected area where a fire was blazing. They set Noël down on a clearing covered with tarpaulin and wrapped her in a thick fur coat. She slipped on some oversized mittens and then someone brought her a cup of steaming broth while a medic knelt down beside her to check the wound beneath the blood and matted hair. Noël grimaced slightly at his touch but did not cry out. Instead she asked, "When can I see my friend Mr. King? I want to thank him for saving my life."

The medic looked sympathetically down at the little girl and smiled. Before he could tell her that her friend was gone, she looked up, stared straight into his eyes and said very seriously, "I know you don't think he's alive, do you? But you'll see. He is a great man and he can't die now. He must live and tell his story to the world. You will see!"

The medic felt like humoring the child but something about her voice and manner was so convincing that he just nodded his head and continued to treat her head wound. A few minutes later Noël and the medic heard a commotion coming from the direction of the makeshift morgue. Two men were moving quickly along a path toward the shelter.

"What's going on?" the medic inquired.

"The guy we found with the girl, he's still alive," he puffed, catching his breath as steam surrounded his face in the frosty air. "We left him with the other bodies but when we returned we found he had moved. Not much, but we could see drag marks in the snow."

The medic looked down at Noël who was smiling quietly with a hint of an I-told-you-so triumph in her expression. He knew he couldn't think about that, for he had to finish up with her and attend to his new patient who was just arriving on a stretcher. The blue bag in his frozen hand was bumping along the ground as the rescuers swiftly approached. They placed the stretcher on the tarpaulin. Noël could see only the stiff arm holding the blue bag as it protruded from beneath the heavy furs that covered the body.

"Oh, how wonderful!" Noël laughed as if everything were okay. "Mr. King saved my bag."

"Your bag?" the medic questioned. "What's he doing with your bag and why is it so important?"

"It's got my gift in it. The one I got from the leader of the people on the other side of the world. It means they want peace just like we do and I must get it to the President of the United States."

"Oh," he said, without the slightest idea of what she was talking about. "Well, I'll get it for you as soon as we can pry it loose from your friend's hand."

"You will take good care of Mr. King, won't you, mister? 'Cause he's my friend and he's hurt."

"Oh yes, dear, don't you worry. We'll fix him up good as new," the medic said, trying to placate the child.

"I don't think you'll be able to do that — only good enough so he can do what he has to do," Noël said in a matter-of-fact tone.

The medic got up, shaking his head in dismay as he moved over to the stretcher. "Strange kid," he said. "The head wound must be causing some kind of hallucination. The doctors will need to take a closer look at her back at the hospital."

The medic knelt down beside my motionless body. He removed the furs and felt around the upper body, finding the severe break in my frozen arm. My face was untouched and my other arm appeared to be intact. He continued his investigation and couldn't find any obvious signs of bleeding. Then he started on my legs and found that both of them were terribly crushed just below the knees.

"God!" the medic exclaimed to the two men who had brought my body to the shelter. He looked at the mangled limbs and shook his head. "This poor fellow's a mess. I can't do anything for him here except apply tourniquets and give him a strong pain killer if he comes around. Now that the weather has started to clear, you can radio for the evacuation chopper to come in and pick up these two survivors as soon as possible. They should be able to land in about an hour when the sun comes up. Let's wrap this guy up tightly and get him prepared for the trip."

"I want to go with my friend Mr. King," Noël said, as the medic and the two rescuers began firmly strapping furs around my body and the stretcher.

"I think we can arrange that, honey. He'll need a friend like you when he wakes up."

17

THE SACRIFICE

WHEN I OPENED MY EYES, I WAS NO LONGER SITTING IN THE AIR-plane next to the disabled man. Instead, I found myself on a flat boulder gazing out onto a calm ocean beneath a cloudless sky. As I watched the blue-green water heave and swell in perfect rhythm, I sensed a force of unimaginable wisdom, love and power gently guiding it. The feeling was similar to the tranquillity of the dreamlike state I had just enjoyed. Despite the horrible final scenes, I felt lighter than air and was in a wonderful state of release. Nothing, it seemed, could take me out of my center of peace, for a greater power controlled the direction of my thoughts. It was a guiding power, benign and vast in its all-encompassing strength and holding a depth of wisdom richer and fuller than could possibly be described. It drew me to a point of creative light so magnetic and all-inclusive in its scope that I could feel only an overwhelming love for all that was or ever could be. I knew beyond any doubt that all was one.

I spoke within myself to the guiding point of light. "Show me what to do for my highest purpose and I will follow."

As I sat blissfully waiting for a sign, I sensed a warm and familiar presence behind me. It was not necessary to turn and look, for a new awareness had been added to my normal vision. It told me my friends were near and with them the guidance I had just asked for.

"You are correct, dearheart," my beloved Sister Diana confirmed. Spirit uses whatever instrument is most proficient to accomplish Its purpose. Our love for each other is very deep and it yields a pure channel through which Spirit can manifest."

I turned and greeted my friends. Their faces were glowing with profound humility and love as they enjoyed the fruits of their labors — my new level of awareness. As before, we strolled along the beach together. Soon Adrian spoke to the matter at hand.

"You have been shown many truths about yourself, about life and about the possibilities of humankind. Your mind has been opened to the great need for guidance in the world at this time. And you have seen the critical work of the wayshowers.

"For many years we, your friends and helpers, have been privileged to guide your footsteps to the threshold of the work you have come to do. All else that has been accomplished in your life has been only a series of stepping stones toward the work that lies before you. And now, at the moment of accomplishment, we are once again blessed by being able to inaugurate you into the humble band of wayshowers. You will join with us in the work of spreading light to a despondent humanity on the eve of the world's great transition into its true reality."

I quietly listened, fully content to allow my life to evolve in whatever direction Spirit had in store for me.

"As on your Earth plane, dearheart," Sister Diana said, "there are many levels and degrees of growth and accomplishment possible. Often in the early stages of inner service on the material plane, it is imperative that the subtle and insidious danger of spiritual pride be eliminated by the camouflaging of your higher attainment and status. That way you are not fully aware of who you are or what you have become. You act largely on a powerful faith that emanates from deep within your soul. That faith is born of a depth of knowing and awareness based on firsthand experience such as you have received. Yet because of this initial cloaking of the mind, you will not understand why your faith is so strong. You will know simply that it is."

Sister Diana fell silent and allowed me to absorb her meaning. It dawned on me that in the work I was about to do, I would be alone, without the benefit of my dear companions to lean upon if things got rough.

Adrian saw that I was getting their point and continued the lesson. "It is an unfinished work that allows the refiner's metal to go untested. The steel must be put to the test before it can be fashioned into a powerful double-edged sword, a sword that becomes both the defender of truth and the separator of all that fails to meet the perfect standards of Spirit's truth.

"The years spent in the Earth school are but the blink of an eye in the expanse of eternity, and while the trials and suffering endured by most of humankind seem to last a long time, in reality they are as fleeting as a summer shower and just as life-enhancing. To set an example of courage and leadership in combination with the bearing of one's own personal suffering with grace and silence offers tremendous inspiration to others.

"You, my friend, are poised on the precipice of a wonderful opportunity — an opportunity to return to the Earth school in a broken body, bearing the message of hope you now possess. The world cries out for this message and the proof that it is not a hollow hope."

I felt a thread of anxiety and doubt pass through my heart as Adrian painted a picture of the choice that lay before me. I realized deep within that the choice was mine and that I need not accept it. There were many other opportunities to serve and I could refuse this one without the guilt associated with the Earth plane. There was an eternity ahead. No one would think less of me if I backed away from this great challenge and sacrifice. The broken, half-frozen body being flown from the crash site on the mountainside need not regain consciousness if that was what I decided should happen. Or the plan for my life on Earth could be fulfilled, the full tree of my life could come to a glorious and perfect fruition in the service of humanity. Only I could make the difficult choice.

In the company of my beloved friends and mentors, strolling happily along the soft sandy beach in an idyllic rapture I could not previously have even suspected existed, the choice seemed remote and unreal. And yet I had to choose.

A terrific force, an almost irresistible magnetic pull within myself demanded that I take the giant leap from dormant, unlimited potential to magnificent accomplishment. I knew I could withdraw, remaining in tranquillity for an eternity if I so willed it. Or I could put aside the heavenly bliss for a time, step back down the great stairway of illumined consciousness and reach out a loving and helping hand to those who cried out for love's gentle embrace.

I knew there really was no decision to be made. How could I do anything but instantly embrace the magical moment and get on with it? What was it that blocked me?

As usual, Sister Diana crystallized my concerns at precisely the correct moment. "A person clings to the illusions that fear generates and, with that intense focus, magnifies the beast he himself has created. True were the words spoken by a man inspired: 'We have nothing to fear but fear itself.'"

I closed my eyes and took a slow deep breath. Until my task had been completed, it was the last breath I would enjoy in the tranquillity and beauty I had shared with my friends.

18

THE VALUE OF SUFFERING

A SEARING PAIN SHOT THROUGH MY BRAIN AS FAINT STREAKS OF light penetrated my swollen eyes. The pain became a throb as my eyelids flickered open. I could see only a foggy white blur and gray shadows that moved around me.

I opened my mouth to speak but nothing would come out. I tried again and managed a strangled croak followed by violent coughing. I guessed that the foggy vision was disorienting my sense of balance because I could not be certain if I was lying down or sitting up. I was also confused about who I was and where I might be. It was as if I had just been born into a strange new world and lacked the abilities to perceive it. Nevertheless, somewhere deep within the recesses of my clouded mind there was a strange sensation of protective tranquillity, a distinct feeling that all was well.

I ceased my struggle to speak and although the throbbing continued, I focused on making out the shadows around me. Moments later I began to get results. After several rapid blinks followed by a few tight squeezes of my eyelids, I started to see distinct images. It became obvious that there were several people around me but for some reason no one was speaking. In fact, there was no sound at all except a fuzzy ringing like the sound of a school bell heard through a thick pillow.

I had become aware that my body was not responding to my mental commands, but that okay feeling was still with me — in fact, it was even stronger than it had been before. Clearer vision was beginning to return and I could just make out a pair of white-uni- formed people in front of me. Judging by the angle of my view, I seemed to be propped up in bed.

As time passed, I began to feel the strange sensation of being imprisoned in some fashion I could not put my finger on. I was mentally exploring the unusual feeling when I heard what sounded like clapping hands echoing far off in the distance. It continued for some time and I tried to turn my head to make out the source of the sound. It was then I realized my neck was held firmly in place by some unseen force. The clapping continued, coming from a differ- ent direction and gradually becoming louder and closer.

A moment later I had a violent spasm of coughing followed by the clear sight of a nurse standing at the foot of my bed. While I was certain I did not know her, I was struck by her familiar appearance. That momentarily distracted me from the sequence of awakening sensory experiences I was experiencing. My croaking voice was slowly beginning to form audible sounds. "Where am I? Who am I? Why am I here? How did I get here? Why can't I move?"

Although my questions were normal under the circumstances, she just smiled with a look that betrayed that she knew something I apparently did not and was very happy indeed about whatever it was. That was a mystery I would have to pursue at a later time since I was distracted by someone shouting.

"Hello, Mr. King. Thanks for saving my life!" The voice came from somewhere to my right and out of my restricted range of vision. The loudness of it indicated the person must have thought I still couldn't hear properly. It was obvious to me that I could hear almost normally and I was thankful, despite the increased throbbing that filled my entire head. It was the voice of a little girl and she seemed to know me. I was wishing I could turn my head to see who was speaking when a strange thing happened. Within my mind I heard, as clear as a bell — in fact, more clearly than I had just heard the child speak — a voice that said, "Don't wish, Jonathan. Will!"

It was a unique sound, not at all like the musing of my own mind when it spoke to itself. It was like listening to someone nearby except that the voice was being generated within my mind instead of coming from outside and entering through the normal channel of my ears.

For a moment I couldn't decide whether to focus my attention on hearing the voice again or on obeying the powerful instruction I had just received.

Although I could not remember who I was, the essence of my character remained. I knew I had led a life of balanced order, meticulous precision and disciplined focus, and those instincts took over. The instruction seemed like commonsense guidance, wherever it had come from, so I willed myself to turn and see who had spoken. To my great surprise the exertion I expected would be required to conquer the restrictive hold on my movements was almost instantly overcome and I turned my head with little effort. I was shocked to see an aging but vibrant woman in the bed next to mine. Bandages covered the entire top of her head. I couldn't believe it! Had my hearing been playing tricks on me?

She smiled the sweetest smile I could remember seeing and nodded her head. Suddenly the room seemed to disappear and the two of us were enveloped in a gentle mist that radiated utter serenity. A moment later I found myself getting up out of the bed and joining the woman as we walked toward each other and she took my hand. I felt a warm pulsating feeling creep up my arm and slowly engulf my entire body.

Then I looked into her eyes and it all came back to me — the walks and the talks with Adrian and Sister Diana, the plane crash, and her, the old woman who had been a child. Even Adrian's assistant in the recovery room after I had bumped my head in the aircraft lavatory . . . yes, the nurse at the end of the bed was Cindy! And the woman was Mother Noël.

Then I understood why she was smiling. Mother Noël had said nothing, allowing me to absorb all that had transpired since I had made my decision to return to my broken body and assume the vital role I was soon to play. I thought of the last words Sister Diana had said to me, the words that had been the needed catalyst for my decision to return. But something was wrong. She and Adrian had talked of the sacrifice of returning to a broken body, yet there I was, feeling vitally alive and whole.

I glanced at the gentle old soul who stood beside me. She was still smiling knowingly as the confused images passed through my mind. She indicated with her eyes that I should turn around. I felt a slight anxious moment then but remained peaceful and secure in her presence. Turning, I saw the two beds, side by side. But there was a little girl in one, and in the other was someone who looked like me.

The hair was matted from lack of grooming. The face was black and blue with multiple bruises and tiny cuts. The eyes were swollen shut. The lips too were swollen and cracked. A long ugly gash was stitched shut across the entire width of the chin. The neck was held firmly in place by a brace connected to several shiny metal arms pushing up against a chin support on the top and a shoulder harness on the bottom.

The left arm was missing completely from just below the shoulder, while the right arm seemed unharmed except for a few lacerations and dark bruises.

White hospital sheets covered the body from the waist down. I felt compelled to stare at what lay beneath the tight sheets. Nothing was there. Slightly above what would have been knee level the thick bulges beneath the sheets ended, leaving only a few crinkled ridges in the neat white cloth.

I detected no life emanating from the eyes, nor any movement in the body, which seemed to be in some kind of suspended state. I looked over at the little girl who seemed calmly aware of my gaze and very much alert. Then I looked back at Mother Noël.

"Records state that both St. Francis of Assisi and St. Paul were seen in two separate places at the same time," she said. "There is no mystery. When we are consciously one with Spirit, which is everywhere, we can manifest when and where it suits our purposes. You might compare it to a diamond with many facets. Still one in its essential nature, it can shine the light through its many windows simultaneously."

My inner sense told me I was between two planes of existence and that a gentle transition was taking place so that much of the trauma of returning to a terribly disabled body would be eliminated.

"Much work is done in the unseen realms where Reality exists, my brother. As you now know, the physical is but a shadow of the true life, the effect of a much greater cause.

"In special cases we are permitted to smooth the discordance associated with disaster and tragedy when the purpose of those challenges is to serve both the soul involved and humankind. Had this been a balancing of the scales of cause and effect or a specific opportunity for you to learn a lesson, our involvement would be very different and totally unseen by you.

"But because as you are here to serve a particular purpose as a newly awakened wayshower, your awareness is almost complete and you are permitted to see some of the work we do for the world in the unseen."

When Mother Noël had finished speaking a corridor magically opened in the mist. She stepped into it and I followed. A moment later the two of us were standing in the corner of a patient's private hospital room. In the single bed was a very old woman who had tubes connected to her arms, her abdomen and her throat. A nurse was busy making an entry in a log book on one side of the bed, and on the table in front of her was a machine monitoring the woman's heart and brain activity.

Mother Noël stepped over to the bed and placed her hand on the old woman's forehead. Instantly, there was a pulsating, radiant white light around her hand and around the entire upper portion of the old woman's head.

Mother Noël moved back to my side and waited patiently. Moments later the woman sat up. That is, part of her sat up. The physical replica of the sitting woman still lay motionless on the bed, but the sitting woman swung her legs over the side of the bed and almost jumped off. She stood silently for a few seconds, testing her newfound strength, then walked over and sat down in a nearby chair.

Mother Noël smiled down at her and nodded her head in greeting. The old woman returned a friendly hello to us both. I greeted her awkwardly, not certain of the proper conduct in such circumstances. My guide turned to me, still smiling, and said, "Love has no code of conduct, my brother. You have only to unselfishly express what is in your heart in the way that feels most comfortable. Remember always to let the love itself do the actual work as it flows through you."

"How could love do the work?" I wondered. "Wasn't I or whoever was loving doing the work?"

"No, my friend! Of ourselves we are nothing but channels, conduits purified by illumination through which love may flow, directed by wisdom and energized by power. In that way we are co-workers with Spirit, whether on this side or on the physical side.

"The difference is that the physical offers many distractions, or temptations, if you like, and those distractions fan the flames of the illusion of limitation. But when a person removes those rose-colored obstructions from his consciousness, the simplicity of the universe becomes visible and he becomes aware that all things are possible and that they always have been."

I considered her words respectfully. Then I looked back and forth from the woman on the bed to the one sitting peacefully in the chair.

"Has she died? I mean passed over," I asked sheepishly, wondering if I was being offensive.

"No, my brother, she has not. And you may ask any question you wish. That is part of your purpose for being here — to clear the confused pockets of doubt still remaining in your mind."

"If she has not passed over, then what has happened?" As I asked the question the nurse looked up at the heart and brain wave monitors and judging by her alarmed reaction, I assumed a serious change had taken place. She pressed a large red button on the wall and hurriedly left the room.

Then it came to me and I blurted out, "She's just gone into a coma, hasn't she?"

"Yes," Mother Noël replied simply. No further elaboration was given. I had learned that silence in a new area of understanding usually meant I must work out at least part of the answer myself. I considered what had happened and what it might mean. I could see that the true identity of the old woman as she sat in the chair was relaxed. She seemed to be comfortable and not suffering in any way I could sense. So why stay between worlds?

Then I thought about my own lengthy sojourn between planes of existence and realized that for me, the purpose had been training and enlightenment. But what did the woman need to learn that at her advanced age could not better be acquired on the other side of pain, debility and suffering in a worn-out garment of flesh?

Suddenly the answer struck me like a bolt: The lessons were not for her. She was to be a catalyst for others' learning experiences.

"Correct," came the soft reply. "You have removed human reason, my brother, and allowed the higher faculty of intuitive guidance to lead you to the answer. So many souls on Earth would find many of their daily trials reduced or eliminated if they would listen for and obey that powerful channel to perfect truth."

My new friend began elaborating on the value of the old woman's remaining in a coma instead of passing over immediately. It seemed that during recent years the woman's only daughter had ignored her failing condition, annoyed by the inconvenience of having to spend her time with a decrepit old woman whose days were numbered. She resented even the few hours expended in visiting her mother's hospital bedside.

Throughout the years the woman had given the best she could to her daughter and like many average families they had led a rather unspectacular, routine life. As the child grew to adulthood, she grasped hold of the brass ring denied her during her youth and pursued a faster lifestyle. In that lifestyle there had been many disappointments and much disillusionment, but despite those challenges she had failed to reach the chastened, humble state that often followed a lifestyle satiated by overindulgence. However, deep down she was not far from that receptive state of mind.

The opportunity to help lift her daughter onto the final steps of that important stage of enlightenment had been given to the old woman, not on the conscious level but on the higher level of true Reality. She had seized the chance and was waiting to see that particular aspect of illusion slip from the mind of her beloved child.

Soon the daughter would become aware of her mother's condition. Gradually, in silence and remorse, she would remember the enduring moments of selfless love her mother had shared with her during the simpler life of her childhood. In shame and humility she would reach out with her heart and soul for help, not for herself but for the return and healing of her dear mother. And in that selfless, humble, prayerful state, a door to her own enlightenment would open.

After Mother Noël had concluded her explanation, she motioned for me to follow her through the foggy corridor that had opened once again. That time the corridor led into a completely different environment. We were in a long open ward with many beds. The room was obviously in a very old building and had a spectacular vaulted ceiling painted with many beautiful images. Several patients groaned in agony. As we walked down the long aisle between the beds I gathered that a major disaster had recently occurred, as most of the patients had sustained serious injuries. We could see a multitude of broken limbs, blood-stained bandages, dark bruises, tourniquets and temporary splints as we reviewed the results of the carnage.

Mother Noël was absolutely calm. As I stood watching, an intensely glowing violet light began to radiate around her and fill the entire room. The cacophony of wailing seemed to lull into a gentler hum, still deeply sad but definitely less heart-wrenching. Presently the chaos and emotionally charged atmosphere began to subside.

Then I felt a powerful magnetic presence behind me. I turned with anticipation and saw a parade of white-cloaked figures filing into the long room. The members of the procession filled the room, unseen by the attending doctors and nurses as they moved methodically toward their goals. When they reached the first set of beds two broke off and proceeded to the nearest patients. The precise activity continued until each injured person had a white-cloaked figure beside him. It was as if an invisible vital force had slowly seeped into the room, giving it an uplifting vigor.

Some of the cloaked figures simply sat and held the hand of a sleeping patient, while others performed an unusual massage about a half inch or so above the person's body, sweeping their hands back and forth. I noticed the dark and muddy colors surrounding the patients who received the treatment slowly build in luminosity and brightness.

Still other figures seemed to overshadow the healing activities of the attending doctors and nurses. When that occurred, the doctors and nurses appeared more dynamic, confident and in control. I stood transfixed, watching patient after patient receive invisible treatment through the servicing attendants.

"In the village below this structure, which rests on a hill commanding a beautiful view of a crystal clear lake beyond, there are several hundred peasants joined in silent prayer," Mother Noël explained. "They are simple people whose possessions are few but whose faith is great indeed. Many hundreds of years ago this structure was part of an abbey formed by the Great White Brotherhood and Sisterhood of which Sister Diana, Adrian and I are privileged to be humble members.

"Although much has been lost of the original teachings and beautiful truths of those days, there still remain a simplicity of life and a faith in the mythical legends handed down from generation to generation. What you are witnessing is a natural law that humankind has been taught for two thousand years, yet few have really comprehended the powerful truth in the simple words: Ask and it will be given unto you.

"Quietly, patiently, unselfishly praying for their injured brothers and sisters, those humble souls have opened the door to a service that my brothers and sisters here are privileged to give to these poor stricken villagers, for it is written that in serving we will be served. The link between those who have gone on a little further in understanding and those devoted souls in the village below will work its magical healing for these disaster victims. It is a link of love that will quickly restore life and vitality and reduce suffering in ways no physical healing service could duplicate.

"You have heard the expression 'As above, so below,' which is represented by the two intersecting triangles known to us as the six-pointed star of the Great White Brotherhood. That is Reality. Yet the natural evolution of that universal law is slowed to a snail's pace by the misguided use of human free will. By listening, as you have learned to do, to your higher intuitive guidance and then in humble obedience following that guidance, the 'below' becomes the 'above' almost instantly. That is the correct use of your free will, and there is a reality more abundantly full of life and love and peace than any on Earth have imagined that opens to a Soul who chooses to follow that simple truth.

"Now there is one last facet of the diamond we want you to look through, my brother. To do so, you must have implicit faith in all that has gone before. You must use the guidance you have been given as the bedrock upon which to build a perfect vehicle that will allow your life's work to begin."

I listened with slight anxiety as Mother Noël prepared me for the final mystery, one that, I gathered, must hold even greater secrets of power than those I had learned so far. My mind raced back to the moment when I had first met Adrian as he had cordially introduced himself during the ill-fated flight. It seemed like eons of time had passed since that friendly greeting and yet very little time had elapsed on the physical plane. I had been held in a suspended vortex of time's illusionary reality, moving backwards and forwards as easily as I might have if I'd been a child playing Simon Says. The confining boundaries of space had dissolved and I had moved with no conscious awareness of obstacles. My friends had helped me to break the fetters of time and space, showing me a universe in which everything existed in the now.

I could not explain it. I could not justify it. I could not argue it. But deep within the recesses of a newly awakened part of me, I knew it to be true. And that truth had set me free. What marvelous secret awaited me I could not begin to guess, but whatever it was, the adventure had become irresistible and I felt alive, invincible, even immortal. I felt ready to conquer worlds, ready to slay dragons, ready . . . for what? Speaking? Inspiring crowds? Was that all I was to do? Why could I not do as I had seen the white-cloaked army of healers do? What was the value of speaking words when that magnificent healing work was needed all over the world? Great human suffering was going on at every moment. Surely that was a more significant calling. . . .

"You have no doubt heard the saying 'Give a man a fish and you feed him for a day; teach him how to fish and you feed him for life.'"

I acknowledged that I had indeed heard that piece of wisdom and counted it as one of my favorites. "Is that the lesson you want to impart to me?" I asked, a little disheartened, for I thought I already knew about the subject.

Mother Noël smiled sweetly at me as an understanding parent would smile at a cocky little child who had bragged about how smart he was when he had learned only elementary facts. I could tell by the kindly look of patience on her face that I had jumped the gun, and I felt embarrassed, so I sheepishly lowered my head and awaited her guidance.

Silence followed as the old woman waited for me to ease out of self-criticism into genuine humility, the wondrous door to wisdom, love and power. Finally, when she felt her student had reached the initial state of receptivity, she proceeded with the final chapter of my lessons, the last of the teachings before my work was to begin.

19

AWAKENING

I FOLLOWED MOTHER NOËL THROUGH THE DOOR AT THE END OF the long infirmary and once again we entered the tunnel of fog. I sensed that something very different awaited me on the next journey.

An incredibly powerful magnetic energy emanated from the interior of the tunnel, and the walls radiated a soundless yet vibrant hurricane of swirling colors. There was nothing ominous about the activity but the chaotic movement of color and mist roaring silently around us was at first unsettling. The disturbing feeling quickly left me as I began to hear a faint but distinct echo of beautiful choral singing. I could not make out its location as it reverberated from some distant, hidden chamber in the interdimensional gateway.

Soon majestic voices thundered like velvet through the corridor. Angelic music penetrated my heart and lifted my soul to a height I had never before experienced. No music, no sound, no choir on Earth could match even one note of that magical symphony in its perfectly unified expression of love.

The walls of the tunnel disappeared. My companion vanished. My body melted into nothingness and only my mind and soul remained, reveling in the rapture of color and music. The color and the music were one. No combination of artists and musicians could have expressed the essence of color and music with more perfect harmony. It was a pastel symmetry. Even the divisions between notes and colors had disappeared into a single expression. It was as if an entire symphony had blended with the total spectrum of color in a single perfect note which was then experienced in an instant.

The effect was overwhelming. It was exquisite, but I was beginning to feel a strain on my nervous system. It was almost as though mild electrical stimulation had intensified to a point where it had become painful. I could take no more.

As I projected that thought, I instantly found myself back in the tunnel with Mother Noël who radiated a knowing smile of welcome. "You have touched the Face of Spirit, Jonathan," she said reverently.

I was speechless. All I could do was reflect on the unimaginable experience I had just gone through. Just before the nervous tension had forced me to let go, I had felt myself joining a glorious oneness with the color and music. I was the color and I was the music, in complete simplicity and truth. It left me with an unshakable knowledge that all was one, manifesting itself through an infinity of expressions.

I could feel it! I knew it! I was it! It was no longer a matter of belief or faith. I had lived through the experience of oneness and knew it to be the truth. No longer could I look at anyone — or anything — and think of him as being separate from myself. He might be different in his manner of manifesting Spirit, yes, but separate? No. That was the beauty of unity in diversity.

For centuries theologians of every description had said in different ways that Spirit is oneness, but most people had no real concept of what that truly meant. If they had, all acts of prejudice would have disappeared from the face of the Earth hundreds of years earlier. Color differences, intellectual distinctions, division of land into nations by invisible lines, fences around whole systems of belief — all were artificial creations of an ugly, painful legacy of fear steeped in separation.

I caught myself chuckling at the vision of a hand condemning its own toe because of its location on the body and its different shape and function. Then I considered the complete absence of the foot from the whole and the serious loss to the body it would represent.

It was all so simple. So clear. How had it escaped me before? I couldn't understand how I and most of humanity had failed to see the indestructible and essential link among all that was seen and unseen, all that was known, imagined or ever thought of — and all that was.

From that moment on, life was to me an infinite sea of spiritual substance, mostly unseen yet always one in its basic nature. Here and there it would pour itself into the mold of a thought that soon became a living entity. The shapes and densities of those new expressions of life would encompass limitless variables, but always the same indivisible and perfect essence would empower and animate those lives.

And through the infinite spectrum of life projected into manifestation by thought, the Spirit within would know Itself. At every level of existence, the perfect harmony of Its being would balance the profusion of life forms and peace would prevail. In this purpose of unimaginable proportion there was constant and simultaneous awareness of all Its parts. It was, therefore, omnipresent, omnipotent and omniscient.

The crowning achievement in the loving heart of the one Source was humankind in whom every facet of Its being was duplicated, even Its free will. Thus, the omnipotence of Spirit was governed by the choices made by the human being. He could listen to Spirit's perfect guidance through his intuition and create peace, or he could obey his lower impulses and create chaos. Spirit would manifest in the direction of a person's thought. That perfect pattern of life had been given to the perfect being called the human so that infinity upon infinity of perfectly created, living thoughts could manifest through him.

But a vital link was missing. Eons ago, conscious awareness of his innate perfection became lost through misuse. Without that vital link, the Supreme Being had only the potential to act.

To reestablish that vital link, humanity would have to be

schooled. It would have to experience every level of consciousness on its way to the reawakening of its true perfect nature and its awareness of its unity with the one Spirit. Upon reawakening, it had then only to obey the supreme laws of love to become a master cocreator with its parent.

Another finger of the one Spirit's creative essence had just realized its basic unity with its parent; I had awakened. I had gone the way of countless other souls, finally to be awakened from eons of forgetful sleep, a sleep in separation and limitation that I now realized had been but an illusion.

I visualized the simple beauty of a seed's persistent struggle up through the heavy darkness of soil finally to blossom forth in praise and gratitude to the source of its life. When I applied the same metaphor to humanity I saw that even though a human being's struggle often seemed without direction and many times bordered on hopelessness, something always drew him unerringly upward to his final unfoldment, the illusion of separation forgotten and the beauty of his nature bursting forth in myriad varieties of magnificence to take his eternal and rightful place beside his Creator.

I stood beside Mother Noël and gazed, now with knowing eyes, into hers. They were like warm pools of light that emanated a divine life-giving essence. I understood. I had awakened. I had taken the final sacrificial step before the bud flowered, and I had done it on faith. The powerful influence of love had been given free rein in my heart and that had inspired my return to the Earth school. Not knowing the full extent of the possible suffering I might be required to undergo, I had obeyed the inspiration and through that selfless act, turned the key to the final door of truth.

My heart was flooded with the light I had been at one with, a light I knew would never leave me. And I knew it was time to take my place of honor in the armies of enlightened beings that were showing the way to those who still labored in the darkness of illusion.

I gazed deeper and deeper into Mother Noël's eyes until I was completely swallowed up in them. A sense of disorientation lasted a few seconds and then I found myself looking at the little girl who shared my hospital room. She was smiling at me from the foot of my bed. I smiled back at her, returning the loving vibration to a being who I knew contained the innocence of a child but also the enlightenment of an awakened soul.

She laughed and walked around to the side of the bed. I could not move my head, which was still firmly braced in its protective collar, so the little Noël was obliged to clamber up onto the bed so I could look directly at her. Although her voice was that of a child, her words were those of a wise soul who had helped me over the final hurdle of understanding and led me to my awakening.

"The days and weeks ahead will be a struggle, my brother, but they will give you time to adjust to the work ahead. It is not enough to be aware and obedient. We must also perfect the equipment for service by taking dominion over it, a dominion that the flesh will initially rebel against. Nevertheless, armed as you are with true understanding, you need only direct the force of your thoughts, guided by the one Spirit in perfect childlike faith, and you will quickly see the manifestation of the results you desire."

I understood her words. Almost immediately I felt a distinct suggestion to sleep. The healing process would progress and I would soon join my fellow wayshowers in the critical work ahead. I closed my eyes and swiftly left my body. As I sat in the higher expression of myself, I was greeted by Sister Diana, Adrian and Mother Noël who were radiating intense rose and violet light. A moment later it enveloped me as well and I joined my friends in the pride and love they felt when another soul overcame the limitations of the world.

20

DOORS ARE OPENED

IN THE WEEKS THAT FOLLOWED, I MADE WHAT ANYONE WOULD call a miraculous recovery. From the moment the head nurse and presiding doctor returned to my room, I displayed a spirit of life and well-being that became the inspiration of everyone in the hospital.

Soon I began to insist on being mobilized, whatever discomfort might be involved for me. After much protesting by the medical staff, followed by gentle rebuffing on my part, an ingenious wheel-chair was constructed by a very creative orderly. It was equipped with a viselike brace to wedge my head and back into an immobile position, together with special shock absorbers to cushion bumps that could be dangerous to my delicate condition. The finishing touch was a quiet, smoothly running electric motor that could easily be operated by the touch of a finger.

I made it my business to become acquainted with the young man during his daily visits to care for my bathing requirements. His name was Peter and he was gentle and friendly and had an obvious feeling of deep caring for the welfare of his patients. However, despite his concern for others, he often seemed despondent and he carried a cloud of discouragement around himself. I read it as frustrated ambition.

Instead of drawing attention to the young man's negative outlook, I focused on the uplifting manner in which he always performed his duties. It didn't take long for Peter to respond to a little kindness and encouragement and we soon became good friends. Peter would come to my room whenever he had a break and sometimes even when he was off duty, and he soon became aware of my persistent desire to be up and about. Without instructions from any of the medical staff, he engineered the conversion of a broken-down wheelchair gathering dust in the hospital basement. He even painted the contraption in bright colors that could be spotted from the farthest distances of the hospital corridors. Patients and hospital staff alike would yell, "Here comes the rainbow rider," whenever they saw the vehicle maneuvering around the halls.

Dr. Goldman, the strictly-by-the-book chief surgeon who had operated on my broken body, gave the device a thorough going-over and then had Peter strap him into it in order to check out the ride for himself. After wheeling himself through several cluttered corridors and over many bumps, he satisfied himself that my neck and back would not be in danger of further injury. Even then, Dr. Goldman gave his approval reluctantly and only because he saw that my gentle persistence was wearing down his staff — and himself. I assured the aging physician that he had made a very wise decision, which would greatly enhance my healing process, and I praised his protectiveness as well as his willingness to compromise.

He puffed himself up slightly and gratefully acknowledged my encouraging accolade, which I made certain to pronounce in front of several of his staff members. As he walked away, he turned thoughtfully and said to the orderly, loud enough for all to hear, "Well done, Peter. Come and see me tomorrow before your shift and we'll talk about that ingenious invention of yours. We might find some other pushy patients interested in giving one of those things a try." Dr. Goldman chuckled a little nervously, holding on to his stern facade. Inside, he knew the value of any strong emotion in promoting the will to live.

Peter beamed and replied loudly, "Yes, Dr. Goldman, I'll be there, doctor. Thank you, doctor!" He looked over at me and I grinned mischievously at him and moved my eyebrows up and down quickly. My facial expression was seen by the gathered staff and several of them broke out laughing.

That was how my new life began. Very soon I was the best-known patient in the hospital for I visited other patients with greater frequency than did most of the doctors on their rounds. The aged and lonely with few friends or relatives to visit them, children who had suffered permanent disabilities, amputees, terminally ill patients and even some in the hospital just overnight — I visited them all and became a welcome and anticipated source of upliftment and encouragement.

I'd come wheeling around a corner into a ward full of patients, my neck and head clamped in as stiff as a board, with a silly grin on my face and one sleeve of my housecoat flapping at my side where my arm had been. As I'd ride in, the patients with enough energy to do so would clap and cheer loudly. Amusement and fun to lighten the atmosphere and a warm heart to cheer the soul were my objectives. I would try to fill the room with life, gaiety and encouragement.

My severe injuries and disabilities gave me a significant advantage because they allowed me to relate to even the worst cases in the hospital. The doctors themselves would ask me to visit particular patients when their own skills had failed to bring a healing response or to bring relief to one who was close to passing. My goal, however, was not just to lift the infirm but also to show others that we all have the power to lift others and in those efforts, no matter how small, we ourselves are lifted.

I shared a room with Mother Noël — or little Noël, as everyone else perceived her. The connection we had forged during the aircraft disaster led the hospital authorities to see the wisdom of allowing us to recover in the same room. Her parents had been flown into town and put up at a local hotel by the airline, and they had agreed with the doctors that she might heal more quickly if she stayed with me.

She had remained in the hospital due to a swelling in her head that would come and go mysteriously. The doctors would no sooner recommend surgery than the swelling would stabilize and she would be taken off the danger list. Her condition baffled the doctors, and it continued off and on while I convalesced. She assured me, as I had sensed she would, that the unusual condition would continue so that she could stay nearby and counsel me before my real work began.

The hospital was really alive the day the President came to visit her. She presented him with the little jade amulet from the leader of the people on the other side of the world. The press was there in force, as her fame had spread way beyond the initial coverage given to her trip a few weeks earlier. When news of the crash had reached the world, encouragement had poured in from every corner of the Earth. The united concern for the little girl of love and peace was bringing together people who had been enemies for centuries.

Because I was the one who had saved her, I received nearly equal visibility. The day the President arrived, the press interviewed scores of patients about us and began giving serious attention to "the rainbow rider," as everyone was calling me.

Of course, all of it was part of the plan to put me in front of the world, and Mother Noël counseled me every step of the way. Each evening I would outline the events that had taken place during the day. She would listen patiently and respond with an intimate knowledge of all the details. Her words were always kindly and instructive as she helped me to chisel the rough edges of my newfound work. "It is the small refinement of something great that makes it perfect," she said.

I recalled my early years as an apprentice to a world-famous designer. There was one special day when I learned about excellence. I had proudly displayed a piece of work I was particularly pleased with. The master had immediately torn it up before my startled eyes and said, "Now, my boy, you can begin the real work!" I remembered it as a harsh way of giving me a good lesson when I thought back on that life-changing day, but it had made me dig deeper into the source of my creativity for the very best that was there. And it had taught me to let go of my achievements, no matter how great they might have been. That release from attachment had given me a special kind of freedom I hadn't understood before.

"Only through the unrestricted flow of creativity do we constantly manifest the highest within us, my boy," my mentor had explained. The words came back to me as I saw the value of a life lived simply, holding on to nothing but giving freely with thanks to the one Source of all that is.

When I shared the memory with Mother Noël, she smiled lovingly at me, knowing the new joy I was experiencing as the true value of a past lesson was revealed to me. "It's like a puzzle piece that seems to be meaningless but finally finds its proper spot in a jigsaw puzzle," I told her.

Mother Noël always saw the deepest meaning behind each door I found opening to me and said, "How often humankind rebels at the apparent cruelty of life's many lessons, never realizing the great blessing they could be for his awakening. He thrashes about wildly, trying to escape, and for a time puts off the benevolent guidance that would have shortened his journey into enlightenment. But finally, the pendulum of life must swing back, and with certainty and precision, it returns the wayward soul to his proper course."

The day after the President's visit to Noël, a front-page article appeared in the local newspaper and it was reprinted in a nationally distributed paper the following week. Within hours of its release a television station was asking for an interview with Noël and me. Dr. Goldman okayed the interview, which he requested to monitor so that it did not overtax our strength. When they arrived, I realized the focus of attention had shifted from Noël to me, for they proposed to call the show "Rainbow Rider, Brother of Mercy." The news anchor was an internationally famous reporter known only by the single name Thea. She began by sincerely and tactfully expressing her amazement at my generous and cheerful attitude, despite my significant personal tragedy. Before I could reply, Dr. Goldman interjected and gave a long, pride-filled monologue on my "incredible achievements," as he put it, throughout the hospital. I was grateful for the opportunity to let the work speak for itself.

The interview rolled on for three hours, covering most of my past life as an internationally recognized architect and including the airplane accident and the past several weeks in the hospital. Thea commended me on the excellent example I was setting for other disabled people across the nation. She finished her interview with an address to the viewing audience. "Internationally known architect Jonathan King, alias Rainbow Rider, Brother of Mercy, has clearly illustrated by his great love and kind actions what an individual who has faced personal tragedy can contribute to the inspiration of not just others like himself but of everyone. Can each of us do any less?"

Then she asked one final question. "Jonathan, considering the wonderful results of your volunteer service throughout the hospital, are you considering a change of careers once you are released?"

Noël, who had been sitting next to me and holding my hand throughout the entire interview, looked at me with a knowing grin as I said to Thea, "If there are those who feel what I have to offer would be of value on a broader scale, then when my friend Dr. Goldman here releases me, I would be greatly honored to share what I can wherever and whenever I am called upon to do so."

A cheer arose from the patients and staff gathered outside our room. Thea took the opportunity to ad lib a plug on my behalf. "Well, ladies and gentlemen, you heard Jonathan's offer. I suggest you get in line early because by the sound of it, very shortly this Earthbound angel going to be in big demand."

In my mind, I could hear Mother Noël's laughter at the choice of words regarding my Earthly status.

Three days later the network aired the interview. The next morning, just after Mother Noël and I had finished our breakfasts, Peter came running into our room excitedly, carrying a heavy-looking bag over his shoulder.

"Noël! Jonathan! It's incredible! I mean, you won't believe the response to the television show. Look at all these telegrams!"

"Slow down, my friend," I laughed. "We'd like to hear the rest of your exciting news before we need a third bed in this room for you."

"Oh, I'm sorry. It's just that I'm so excited for you. Dr. Goldman said I could give you two the news and bring down all these telegrams and phone messages. Thanks to you, Jonathan, Dr. Goldman has become my friend and he said it would be okay if I sort of act as your agent while you're still here and screen the calls from all your new fans. Of course, that's if it's okay with you, too?" he asked, an anxious, hopeful look on his face.

I gave him a big grin and raised my eyebrows in what had become my famous silent method of saying yes. He beamed back his delight like a little child and plopped himself down in a chair at the end of my bed so I wouldn't have to move my whole body to see him. He took in a deep breath to calm himself down and then proceeded with the news.

"There are literally hundreds of messages of encouragement and good wishes here for both of you. They're from all over the continent and even from other countries that picked the show up on satellite. The heads of several disability organizations want to use you in their fundraising campaigns and some want you to be their spokesperson. One even went so far as to offer you a seat on its board of directors.

So far, four television talk shows have invited you to appear as soon as you are able and one said they would interview you right here in the hospital by satellite. Three universities want you to speak about human potential and crisis management. And as of half an hour ago, twenty Fortune 500 companies have asked you to address their employees on subjects ranging from courage and inspiration to service and self-motivation.

But the hospital requests are what I've got in just this one bag alone. Peter lifted the ponderous bag up over the railing at the end of my bed and dumped its contents onto the blanket where my legs should have been. Hundreds of telegrams and phone messages dropped from the laundry bag Peter had used and covered the entire available surface of the bed, spilling onto the floor.

I heard Mother Noël in my mind saying, "Well, my friend, you are on your way. And be certain that Adrian, Sister Diana and I will be with you every step of the way!" My heart was full to overflowing as Peter continued.

"Everyone wants you, Jonathan! Everyone! Oh, I'm so proud to have been of some assistance to you and now to be your friend as well. And of course you too, little Noël. None of this would have happened without you. You two have done so much for me and for the hospital, and now you'll be able to help thousands more." Peter was weeping tears of joy as he spoke and Noël and I couldn't help shedding a few tears of our own at the sight of the happy young man who had been so downcast only a few weeks before.

"You must have been screening these messages since early this morning, my friend," I said with appreciation. Something in my words must have triggered Peter's memory and he jerked his head up with a surprised look of concern on his face.

"Gosh, I nearly forgot. There are three people waiting to see you. There were many others and I sent them all away until you had a chance to think about how to deal with all this attention, but there was something very different about these three. They wouldn't tell me what it was about, just that it was a surprise. One of them had a white nun's habit on and was just so kind-looking that I couldn't seem to say no to her. But if you say so . . ."

I cut him off as gently as I could manage and asked him to show them in immediately. Peter was surprised but glad he had not told them to leave. When they arrived, they walked unceremoniously into the room and Peter turned respectfully to leave. I called to him and he turned around. "You have a keen eye, my friend, and you did well to allow my dear friends to remain behind."

Peter beamed with joy and whistled his way out the door which he quietly closed behind himself.

Sister Diana, Adrian and his assistant Cindy embraced me and Noël, who had resumed her adult appearance for the occasion. I was so happy to be with my special friends who had contributed so much to my awakening that I started to weep. They beamed with joy and for several minutes the room was flooded with beautiful living colors.

While I had felt their presence often during the weeks of convalescence, we had not had any actual contact. Mother Noël had explained that it had to do with intensifying the physical healing process by keeping me in a sort of unconscious yet focused state during my sleeping hours.

"I have missed you, my friends, but I have always felt your presence." They smiled and nodded. "You have never been out of our sight since the day of your birth, dearheart," Sister Diana said. "For although Spirit gives no special attention to individuals, much attention is devoted to anyone or anything that can motivate his divine purpose in the world."

"I think you can see clearly, Jonathan, by all that has transpired in such a short time, how much use you can truly be for that purpose," Adrian added.

I humbly agreed. Then I asked about something that was confusing me. "Please don't misunderstand my question, dear friends, but I am wondering why you elected to use normal physical means to visit me when you could have just arrived here whenever you wished to?"

Sister Diana smiled and replied, "What makes you think we did arrive in the normal fashion, dearheart?"

I stopped for a moment. Then Sister Diana's meaning suddenly struck me. "You mean . . . you mean Peter is one of you? I mean, one of us?" I stammered.

"Not yet, my friend, not yet," Adrian answered. "But he is, you might say, an apprentice who needs a master to teach him the finer points of the craft."

My mouth hung open as I absorbed his startling words. It seemed that every time I was with my friends they had some new revelation for me. Was I to teach Peter as they had taught me? Could I be ready for such an undertaking?

"Not quite, Jonathan," Adrian said, "We won't be throwing you to the wolves by having you attempt such an important matter all by yourself. You will assist, and gradually, he will begin to suspect we are more than just your friends as he meets one unexplainable event after another, always in our presence. Your link with him will lift him over the bumps of fear and suspicion and open his mind, allowing us to begin the real work we have prepared for him. By now you have learned that Spirit uses whatever means are at Its disposal to accomplish Its purpose, while never interfering with free will."

I smiled but remained silent, as I felt my friends were there for more than a casual visit.

"You are quite right, dearheart," Sister Diana said. "And now, as you see, the work is about to begin. Because of your disability, you will be in need of assistance once your recovery allows you to leave the hospital, which will be much sooner than the doctors expect. They will attribute your speedy recovery to your zeal for life and keen positive outlook. That will only foster our purpose and spread your international visibility faster.

"Today, we wanted to formally introduce you to Adrian's assistant, Cindy, whom you have already seen a number of times. She will be with you all the way to help you with your physical needs. Peter, as you have correctly observed, has considerable ability and will, in fact, become your agent, as he jokingly put it earlier.

"And we, dearheart, will play our humble part in seeing that the proper doors are opened and that the wrong ones do not divert your attention to your important work."

My head was bowed in thanksgiving. With deep humility I asked my friends and the Great Spirit for the strength to be worthy and capable of successfully carrying out the work ahead. Then Adrian changed the mood by saying, "I'll bet you thought you were going to get rid of us, didn't you?"

Everyone joined in a big laugh, and the atmosphere became charged with creative energy as the conversation moved into an inspiring discussion of plans for the work before us.

21

SHARING THE TRUTH

AND SO BEGAN MY WORK ON A PATH THAT NEVER, IN MY WILDEST imagination, would have occurred to me earlier in my life. I began my mission armed with an awakened consciousness, supported by loving friends and filled with a burning passion to share the truth about the freedom that awaited those who would fill their hearts with love.

Peter did indeed become my agent-producer and, coached by Adrian, laid out a carefully chosen pattern of speaking engagements. The keenly anticipated first event began six months to the day after the plane crash and was handled, again, by Thea, who soon became a close friend of us all, especially Peter. She coordinated a television special with the leader of the people on the other side of the world, the President, myself and little Noël which took place at the nation's capital and featured the story of Noël's journey, details of the airline tragedy, including actual video footage taken by a rescuer, and the miraculous events that had occurred since then at the hospital. The show was beamed by satellite to more than one and a half billion people around the globe, and it ended with the four of us holding our hands aloft in a gesture of peace.

Everyone present laughed as little Noël, on the end, held up my empty sleeve and giggled. Influenced by Sister Diana and Adrian, Noël's parents had agreed to let her accompany me, provided a tutor travel with us. The heart-opening story of Noël's great love for the world and for peace, combined with the challenges I had faced with courage and positive vision, warmed the hearts of audiences wherever we went.

In humble simplicity Noël and I shared our story over and over again. Wherever we traveled, the seeds of love and peace and hope were planted, and they helped to dissolve differences, harmonize discord and foster cooperative communication. No dignitary, politician, theologian or celebrity in the world was better known or better loved.

Religious leaders of almost every persuasion welcomed our living message of truth, usually without the slightest feeling that we were intruding on their personal doctrines. In fact, we would often leave them with a deeper understanding of the truths that lay within the framework of their own teachings.

The years moved quickly toward the end of the century and as it approached, the rapid changes on the planet added urgency to our message. Noël was eighteen years old, in the eyes of the world, and she was a vision of loveliness. The message slowly evolved as we prepared the world for the full significance of the Millennium Tablets. Our story had gradually seeped into the fabric of life, and people were almost ready to understand the full impact of the plan for humankind that had been put into motion so many millions of years before. Gradually, Noël and I began to share with those who were ready to hear it pieces of the spiritual truth that lay behind the illusion of the physical plane. The critical mass of world change grew ever closer and as a result, the power of Spirit flowing through our message became more and more vital.

Always, however, as our message taught, we gave credit to Spirit and illustrated in the truth of our lives that by ourselves we are nothing, that as we let go and allow the wisdom, love and power of Spirit to flow through us, all things are possible and all obstacles can be conquered.

As he worked with us month after month and year after year, Peter became more and more aware of the deeper truths slowly being revealed in our work and of the steps we were taking toward the eventual revelation of the Millennium Tablets. By 1998 Thea, who had been assisting us by using her considerable influence in the media world, had been married to Peter for four years and had joined our worldwide tour as co-producer. Adrian had been a guiding light for her in her collaboration with us and through his deep love, understanding and gentle guidance, he had helped her also to discover much of the truth behind our mission.

Although the light of receptivity was shining ever brighter in the minds of thousands of new supporters who shared our love for humanity, one of the basic truths in the physical world is that for every up, there is an equal down, and for every light, there is an equal dark. My friends and I knew that as our work grew in intensity, and considering the inevitable and dramatic changes occurring in the world during the final years before the millennium, the forces of darkness and resistance would also grow in power.

While the point in history at which the changes would occur had been determined eons earlier, the method of transition was left up to the free will of humankind. The primary objective of our work, therefore, was to let the next thousand years begin on a wave of light, the light I had seen in my visions years before. As in all change, there was the possibility of considerable discomfort, particularly if that change were resisted. Our aim was to help humans to open as fully as possible to their intuition and, through the flood of guiding light and help always available from Spirit during critical turning points, move into the Age of Enlightenment as calmly and gently as possible. Wherever we went, we sought out and encouraged the true seekers of truth in order to help them awaken to the their potential as wayshowers in the new millennium.

The magnitude of spiritual inspiration and energy stimulating the planet grew ever more powerful as time pressed on toward the year 2000, and our efforts were rewarded time and again as many thousands of people awakened and joined Adrian, Sister Diana, Mother Noël and me in our quest. The new lightbearers took up the torch in every corner of the Earth. In their capacities as doctors and teachers, coaches and laborers, politicians and diplomats, kings and queens and humble peasants, in virtually every vocation and character humanity had to offer, people contributed their energy, and the work picked up momentum.

But the elements of fear that led to the greed and misuse of power it fostered were more powerful in the 1990s than at any other period in the history of humanity. When our work had first begun, our inner vision had shown my friends and me a planet in darkness. In those early days, there had been only little pinpoints of light, but they had grown to beacons that were quickly merging together. And with the greater light came a greater clarity wherever the darkness was exposed. The increased clarity also brought a powerful awakening to people as they began to find their previous concepts of reality shattered, with illusion after illusion crumbling before their awakening eyes.

Great hope for the Age of Enlightenment that would follow the end of the century was mixed with a terrible fear of the changes already rapidly sweeping the planet. Millions suffered at the hands of ruthless leaders as their countries were thrown into conflicts motivated by the greed of a few heartless souls. Poverty, homelessness, drug abuse, lust and crime festered like open wounds similar to the ugly sores endured by millions suffering from the new plagues that were more horrible than any ever before recorded.

If that hadn't been enough to terrify humanity, Mother Earth, motivated by her critical role in the Age of Light to come, had cleansed and healed herself in preparation for the birth of her new body. She'd used a multitude of catastrophic earthquakes, mudslides and volcanoes to heal the wounds caused by the physical and emotional pollution with which humans had carelessly poisoned her body over the years. As her lengthy delivery continued, she heaved and sighed in agony, creating winds and floods the likes of which had never been seen before.

Then, just before the turning of the century, working with Spirit, a meteor of enormous proportions rocketed past the planet, cleansing the atmosphere of the sickness that permeated it but causing widespread panic as the weather patterns of the world turned upside down and darkness covered the Earth for three days and three nights.

As the accumulated toxic thoughtforms of centuries manifested their ravaging effects in the physical world and the preparations for a new Earth raged on, we traveled the world with our simple tale of love, courage and hope. In the areas where wars had been fought and the emotions of hatred and vengefulness ran the highest, the process of cleansing was the most severe. In those places we shared the inner secrets of the power of thought and passion and showed those who would listen that they could positively alter if not change the painful circumstances of their lives through their individual and combined efforts.

As the 1990s rolled quickly toward their conclusion, the darkness became pockets and the light became a blanket that surrounded the world. In all but a few stubborn places, containment of the forces of evil had become almost complete in anticipation of the transmutation that would soon arrive. And the heightened consciousnesses of a sufficient number of people were prepared for the full and glorious truth contained within the Millennium Tablets.

Thea and Peter prepared a worldwide satellite linkup and through their media associations, they coordinated everything from giant stadiums, amphitheaters and domes to small-town theatres and meeting halls so that all could receive the message of freedom that Noël and I would soon deliver.

Adrian, Sister Diana, Mother Noël and I had specifically prayed for and projected to this day for several years, while many thousands of other lightbearers had focused on the time of this great revelation for eons.

Our spirits were high and our hearts were full as Noël and I took our places in the studio in preparation for the momentous transmission.

22

THE MILLENNIUM TABLETS

THEA AND PETER WATCHED IN THE CONTROL ROOM AS THE monitor in front of them ran the show's title as a test signal for the satellite linkup around the world. The title read simply, "The Millennium Tablets . . . Revealed."

Five minutes passed and finally the moment we had prayed for and worked toward for years was upon us. The cameraman in front of me gave me a signal to commence and without fanfare I began the address.

> My beloved brothers and sisters, I embrace you in love and light as we share these precious concepts with almost four billion people and deliver our message of hope to all who seek freedom from the bondage of humanity's past.

> As many millions of you with whom we have shared our story are aware, over the past several years, the secrets of the Millennium Tablets have been opened to all humans who have existed since the creation of the universe. Many have been called but few have been chosen to receive the truths hidden within them. Only the truest seekers with the most virtuous and courageous of hearts have ever received the contents of more than the first two basic tablets. The few who

have been privileged to learn those mysteries have gone on before the bulk of humanity and have served throughout its development as wayshowers and light-bearers of the truth contained within the tablets so they could assist humanity in its eventual salvation from darkness. Throughout history they have labored and served, mostly unseen by the world, with deep love and humility, but never have they worked harder than during the past half-century, training those who would join them as apprentices in the final stage of their quest — the quest for the freedom of humanity. I have been honored to be counted among those fortunate enough to assist them in that lofty work.

As you know, the contents of the first tablet have been common knowledge for almost fifty years and many teachers and speakers from around the globe have spread that knowledge in various ways so all could learn. Much of the knowledge, however, was eventually used for selfish acquisition and, as a consequence, it failed to satisfy the user or lead to its deeper purpose — a giant step toward eventual freedom.

I will begin by summarizing for you the twelve concepts of the first Millennium Tablet, as I have done many times before.

The first of the twelve concepts says that every person has the divine power to create. Consciously or unconsciously, everyone creates every second of his life.

The second concept says that every person creates what he wants through thoughts, for thoughts are living things. Unaware of this truth, most people have, therefore, created unconsciously during most of

Earth's history.

The third concept says that a person's thoughts can come through the impulses of his lower nature or through the inspirational intuition of his higher nature. If he is unfamiliar with his link to his higher nature through intuition, he unconsciously creates chaos, an offspring of the selfish character of the lower nature.

The fourth concept says that once a thought has been accepted, in order for it to manifest as a creation it must become a person's objective. Therefore, a person must move the thought from the mainstream flood of daily ideas into the fertile garden of his focused attention.

The fifth concept says that life is a cycle, always moving upward in a spiral. Its first stage is fertilization, the planting of the objective in the subconscious mind. Weak, ephemeral thoughts quickly die because they haven't taken root in fertile soil. That has often saved people from the negative consequences of thoughts having their origin in his lower nature.

The sixth concept says that to breathe life into his creation a person must consistently pour his life force into his objective. That energy can be provided through the lower nature as selfish desire or through the higher nature as love through passion.

The seventh concept says that a person must add activity to his objective and his life force. He must provide a flexible strategy for the growth of his objective into physical manifestation. That, too, can be provided by the concrete mind of his lower nature or by the inspirational guidance of his intuitive higher nature. All of creation must be fed. Without the energy of attention, all a person's creations will expire, no matter what stage of growth they have achieved.

The eighth concept says that there is always a period of waiting, or gestation, during which the objective spends time in darkness. It appears to be a time of inactivity when in reality it is the time of greatest growth. Beware, for it is a dangerous time when a faint heart might withdraw the life force through discouragement and allow the objective to die prematurely. Persistent and consistent focus is essential for the creative objective to germinate, just as the seed that cannot be seen must receive nutrients and water during its growth under the earth.

The ninth concept says that the mold of the objective to be materialized must be strong and of a definite shape. A person must hold steadily before his inner eye a vision of his objective as it will eventually appear. Visualization of the objective's eventual manifestation draws to it, like a magnet, the circumstances necessary for its successful fruition.

The tenth concept says that the birth of the objective can occur according to a person's strategy or of its own nature, as all creations are cells in a larger creation often unknown to humanity. Herein lies a deep mystery to be revealed in another tablet. It may be said, however, that the thought forms of a group can assist, impede or eliminate the thought forms of an individual. Therefore, a person must consider timing in his choice of objectives, as the tide of events or group thoughtforms might be against the likelihood of his success. Conversely, he must be alert to the opportunity of focusing on an objective whose time has come due to the same group forces.

The eleventh concept says that after birth, the next stage of creation is death, for death is really a part of the cycle of life, which constantly repeats itself. All good that is past its time becomes evil. Heed well the clue hidden in this concept, for it has deep and healing significance. Nothing more is permitted to be said in this tablet about the subject except that a person would do well to observe Mother Nature closely and see the truth concerning this part of life's cyclic activity.

The twelfth concept says that after death, the next stage of creation is decay back to the source from which the thought began, thus completing the upward-spiraling cycle. The advice of concept number eleven applies here, too.

Once again, my sisters and brothers, we have shared the truths of the first tablet. As we study these twelve concepts we can see, by looking through the pages of history, how most of the people endowed with these powerful truths have misused them for selfish purposes. However, we must not sit in judgment, for Spirit has always had a master plan that most people do not see. People have sometimes grown through temporary excess and selfish overindulgence, although that method of evolution has been the most painful.

In these last several years of the century enormous strides have been made toward the positive and proper use of these creative powers as the secrets hidden within the second Millennium Tablet have been revealed to, assimilated by and employed by more and more of humanity's true seekers — many of whom actually reached their current level of genuine humility through the consequences of misusing the first twelve concepts.

And now it is my sublime pleasure and deep honor to introduce to you my partner and colleague, Noël, who will deliver to you the contents of the second Millennium Tablet. I give you Noël.

My fellow seekers of truth, I come to you today with a heart that is overflowing with love and gratitude to the Great Spirit for all that has been given through love. As we approach the final step before the millennium and the Age of Enlightenment and peace we encourage you to look back on human history as a preschool education. During our impressionable early growth we, the children, have often rebelled against a strange and unfamiliar world that was frequently cruel and uncaring.

We must not blame our predecessors for teaching us poorly, for they only passed on the experience of their own existence and in most cases they did the best they could. It may seem regrettable that much of humanity's growth has been through suffering in darkness, but once again consider the critical root system developed by a beautiful flower as it toiled blindly through the darkness toward the light and warmth of the sun.

And now at this auspicious time, a time foretold for

eons as the graduation of humankind into the light, I am privileged to open the seal of the second Millennium Tablet and pour out its healing oils of truth to all of humanity. I have also been commissioned to take you a step further, that you may see what the immediate future holds for all who lovingly pursue these truths.

And so, my beloved brethren, I give you the second Millennium Tablet.

The first of the twelve concepts says that the human being is more than a creator; he is a cocreator with the Great Spirit. Therefore, all things are possible to him.

The second concept says that a human being has total and unconditional free will. Therefore, as a cocreator with Spirit, he creates his own circumstances, his own reality, every moment of his existence. Spirit has set the stage and provided Its own law which It must obey. It can neither interfere nor intervene on humanity's behalf under any circumstances unless requested to do so, whether by an individual for himself or for others, or by a group for themselves or for others.

The third concept says that the first step toward a life of harmony and peace is to listen to the wise and loving guidance of Spirit in all creative endeavors. Intuition is the link to that guidance and it runs like a thread through all twelve tablets.

The fourth concept says that in order to progress toward eventual freedom, a person must subdue his lower nature by yielding to the guidance he receives through his intuition.

The fifth concept says that a person has many powers that lie dormant until they emerge at the proper time. These latent powers can be referred to as psychic abilities but are called by many names. The names are of little importance but the abilities are essential tools in the Age of Enlightenment now dawning, much as the five senses have been essential during the dark period of human history to date. The connection to those abilities is through the intuition which bridges the physical senses to them.

The powers now opening to all humankind are these: the ability to communicate mentally with others from a distance; the ability to forecast, through inner sight and hearing, the outline of events that have not yet occurred; the ability to move third-dimensional objects with the mind; the ability to see and read the meaning of the energy fields, or auras, around all living things; the ability to read the past through direct or indirect contact with persons, places or things on the Earth plane; the ability to communicate with all life in both higher and lower dimensions of reality; the ability to heal by acting as a channel for Spirit's life force as it flows through his touch, his words or his thoughts.

The sixth concept says that each facet of the human being has its own body: the physical, including the energy, or etheric, body; the emotional; the mental; and the spiritual. They have been referred to as the aura and as a coat of many colors, and they can be seen when the latent powers are awakened and developed. Thus can a person know what is inside others even as what is inside himself can be known to others. When nothing can be hidden, deceit will end and much suffering will end along with it.

The seventh concept says that from this time on, all of humankind will find these powers quickly emerging and developing as Mother Earth finishes her preparations to make the transition into the next dimension of reality. That reality has been referred to as the Heaven world or Heaven on Earth, a dimension in which humans will walk and talk with the angels.

The eighth concept says that there is no death. The next dimension is where the several bodies of every human have always existed at all times and where they remain when he discards the physical body. In the Age of Enlightenment, there will be no separation from those who have chosen to shuffle off the mortal coil of the physical body.

The ninth concept says that the Earth plane is a school, designed in part to help awaken humankind to its true status in the universe as cocreator with the Great Spirit. This is the time of humanity's graduation to the next level of life's expression.

The ninth concept says that the Earth plane is a school, designed in part to help awaken humankind to its true status in the universe as cocreator with the Great Spirit. This is the time of humanity's graduation to the next level of life's expression.

The tenth concept says that a person must become the truth, not merely understand it. Without activity, thoughts and words are hollow and are powerless to create change. This process takes time, as the human understands time, to incorporate into his being.

The eleventh concept says that there are several key facets in the diamond of truth. A person must integrate these facets into his daily life in order to become the truth. The following are those key facets: understanding, tolerance, patience, compassion, kindness, selflessness, forgiveness of others and forgiveness of self, nonattachment and nonresistance. The last three have been major stumbling blocks for humanity's progress throughout history.

Forgiveness is an incredibly powerful tool, and it leads to freedom. When a person holds others and himself accountable, he holds on to the past. Let the dead bury the dead. The laws of creation, as given in the first Millennium Tablet, ensure that whatever humanity has put into action will return to it in equal measure. There is no escape. The Great Spirit of the universe is exact. But if a person holds on to the past, he perpetuates the original action which then becomes a destructive and repeating pattern that will block his growth.

Attachments to things of the worldly dimension are like garbage bags full of the past. Once a creation has come into the world, it must be set free so its energy can flow to others. That truly is being in the world but not of the world. Instead, a person must lay up his treasures in the Heaven dimension, and those treasures are the facets of the diamond that are indestructible and that are not subject to the laws of the Earthly dimension which cause them eventually to die and decay. As a cocreator with Spirit a person has no need to hold on to that which can be duplicated and improved upon. The fear of loss due to the human being's lack of understanding of his great gift as cocreator has been one of the most significant causes of wars and the death and destruction they have spread on the planet.

Resistance to any worldly circumstance will cause it to remain with a person until that resistance and the life force focused upon it have ceased. What is resisted persists. What is focused on remains alive. Therefore, a person must resist not. He must let go of his control and let Spirit flow through all circumstances he wishes to leave behind, focusing his life force, instead, on those things and circumstances he wants to manifest into his life, not those he does not want.

The twelfth concept says that the path to freedom is through the blending of wisdom, love and power. The first Millennium Tablet teaches the use of power. The second Millennium Tablet teaches the use of wisdom. And the thousand years of peace which are to follow the end of this century will allow humankind the time and experience to germinate these precious seeds in an environment conducive to the integration of love.

And when the three are one in conscious reality, not just in understanding and awareness, then the final salvation of the human being will take place. He will know the truth. He will live the truth. He will be the truth. And the truth will set him free.

The integration will progress through the release, each one hundred years, of another of the Millennium Tablets, from the third Millennium Tablet to the twelfth Millennium Tablet, each tablet containing twelve concepts and together adding up to one hundred forty-four. Each concept will take one thousand years to fully integrate into human consciousness, finally making up the number of the saved — one hundred forty-four thousand.

Now, my brothers and sisters of the Earth, you have the secrets of the first two Millennium Tablets. Many of you have heard most of these concepts through your lives in a thousand different ways. But the knowledge is not enough; you must also have belief in their truth. And once you have the belief, you must have the faith that they will work. And once you have the faith, you must have the knowing based on personal experience. When you know the truth and live the truth, you are the truth, and the truth will set you free.

As we have said, the Millennium Tablets and their mysteries have always been available to anyone who would persistently pursue them with a pure and courageous heart. The greatest stumbling block in humanity's spiritual evolution has been the use of intermediaries who have put themselves between the people and the Great Spirit.

Therefore, take your own counsel. Take what guidance you like from any source you desire but in the end, always filter it through the lens of your own intuition, and the proper direction that is exclusive to your own personal life path will always unfold to you!

Many who are now watching this telecast have achieved the knowledge, and they believe. A lesser number have acquired the faith and have joined in our sacred mission of spreading the information revealed in the first two Millennium Tablets. It is now up to everyone to live the truth during the glorious years of peace just ahead, and eternal freedom will be yours.

My brother Jonathan here and my colleagues just beyond your current vision who have dedicated themselves to the freedom of humankind which they have already achieved, send you light and love and assure you that they are working hand in hand with the Great Spirit and will be with you every step of the way.

I leave you now with the eternal words of one who has been with us since before the world was formed. This same great soul told us that all would do what he had done and do even greater things. "In the world you have tribulation, but be of good cheer, I have overcome the world."

BOOK MARKET

A reader's guide to the extraordinary books we publish, print and market for your enLightenment.

NEW!
THE EXPLORER RACE

Robert Shapiro/Zoosh

In this expansive overview, Zoosh explains, "You are the Explorer Race. Learn about your journey before coming to this Earth, your evolution here and what lies ahead." Topics range from ETs and UFOs to relationships.

$24.95 Softcover 650p

Zoosh through Robert Shapiro

ISBN 0-929385-38-1

BEHOLD A PALE HORSE

William Cooper

Former U.S. Naval Intelligence Briefing Team Member reveals information kept secret by our government since the 1940s. UFOs, the J.F.K. assassination, the Secret Government, the war on drugs and more by the world's leading expert on UFOs.

$25.00 Softcover 500p

ISBN 0-929385-22-5

POISONS THAT HEAL

Eileen Nauman DHM (UK)

Homeopathy is all that remains to protect us from the deadly superbugs and viruses that modern medicine has failed to turn back. Learn how to protect yourself and your family against the coming Ebola virus and other deadly diseases.

$14.95 Softcover 270p

ISBN 0-929385-62-4

◆ BOOKS BY LIGHT TECHNOLOGY RESEARCH

SHINING THE LIGHT

Revelations about the Secret Government and their connections with ETs. Information about renegade ETs mining the Moon, ancient Pleiadian warships, underground alien bases and many more startling facts.

$12.95 Softcover 208p

ISBN 0-929385-66-7

SHINING THE LIGHT BOOK II

Continuing the story of the Secret Government and alien involvement. Also information about the Photon Belt, cosmic holograms photographed in the sky, a new vortex forming near Sedona, and nefarious mining on sacred Hopi land.

$14.95 Softcover 422p

ISBN 0-929385-70-5

SHINING THE LIGHT BOOK III

The focus shifts from the dastardly deeds of the Secret Government to humanity's role in creation. The Earth receives unprecedented aid from Creator and cosmic councils, who recently lifted us beyond the third dimension to avert a great catastrophe.

$14.95 Softcover 512p

ISBN 0-929385-71-3